DO GOOD,
Feel Better

DISCOVER YOUR SOCIAL IMPACT PERSONALITY TYPE TO THRIVE IN YOUR LIFE, WORK, AND COMMUNITY

LAURA WELLS MCKNIGHT

Foreword by Ann-Marie Harrington

AVIVA
PUBLISHING
New York

Do Good, Feel Better: Discover Your Social Impact Personality Type to Thrive in Your Life, Work, and Community

Address all inquiries to:
Laura Wells McKnight
13725 Metcalf Avenue, Suite 316
Overland Park, KS 66223
info@goodcelebrated.com

www.lauramcknightpublishings.com

ISBN: 978-1-944335-37-3

Library of Congress Control Number: 2016919189

Editor: Tyler Tichelaar, Superior Book Productions
Cover and Interior Design: Nicole Gabriel, AngelDog Productions

Published by:
Aviva Publishing
Lake Placid, NY
(518) 523-1320
www.avivapubs.com

Every attempt has been made to source properly all quotes.

Printed in the USA
First Edition

For additional copies visit:
www.dogoodfeelbetter.com

To My Sister

Contents

FOREWORD

You, Made Bold Through Social Impact

I started Embolden in 1998 because I could not resist the window of opportunity to help companies and organizations access the power of the Web to grow their enterprises. I was inspired to make the new technology of the Web accessible and empowering. This meant cutting through the mystery and confusion that always surrounds anything new.

First, I had to learn the technology, from the ground up. Deconstructing a problem was not new to me. I'd never had any formal design training, but I'd always been interested in art, composition, and color. Painting and printmaking were my favorites. I was also trained as a social worker, which meant I'd spent a lot of time figuring out human motivations and behavior. How things work is fascinating to me, from the gadgetry to the communication necessary to explain to others how it works. Left brain plus right brain is how I work best.

In the '90s, when the Web was just taking off, there was no formal training available for building websites. So I taught myself. Companies and organizations needed websites! Embolden began as a web design and digital communications company especially for nonprofit clients and high-growth small businesses. Through the websites we built at Embolden, our clients were instantly empowered to magnify the good they were doing for their customers, employees, and the community as a whole.

With so much demand for websites, Embolden grew rapidly. For seventeen years, we created online platforms of influence so nonprofits could engage donors and for-profit businesses could connect with their customers. Our mantra was "Think. Feel. Do." That is, every website we created was successful if it made visitors think a certain way, feel good about it, and, most importantly, do something. Take action! Whether it was making a gift to a charity or purchasing a product, the action was critical. If a website did not result in action, we had not done our jobs.

Embolden thrived. In 2014, I sold Embolden to Crown Philanthropic Solutions, a provider of cloud-based donor engagement software, where I joined the executive leadership team. Two years later, the owners of Crown sold the company to RenPSG, North America's largest independent provider of philanthropic solutions.

FOREWORD

Throughout the entire journey, a single thread kept my attention. From the very beginning at Embolden, our staff enjoyed spending time with charities and making a difference, or what's now known as "social impact." So it was a no-brainer for me to incorporate "doing good" into our business model. Happy staff equals happy clients equals productive workplace equals making more money. It was a natural part of building a successful business.

As the company grew, however, it became tougher to figure out how to implement a social impact culture (though I didn't know at the time that's what it was called). We were giving a lot of cash to various nonprofits, but it just didn't feel strategic. I was trying to get the staff involved in the decision-making about sponsorships. This was my way of ensuring the dollars were coming full-circle and making a positive difference in our corporate culture, as well as in the community. That was easier said than done. I knew we were doing good, but we weren't capturing it or building on it as well as we could.

Little did I know, halfway across the country, Laura McKnight had left her position as CEO of the Greater Kansas City Community Foundation because she was seeing this trend, too—companies and people wanting to do good but getting stuck on how to recognize and celebrate social impact and keep the momentum going. She saw what I was experiencing with our clients and employees repeated again and again...how the increasing demands of work and life can make it difficult for people to feel like they're making a difference in their personal lives and their companies.

Laura hired a team of researchers to gather data, perform dozens of focus groups, and scour the literature. After years of research, Laura ultimately developed the Social Impact *Personality* Type diagnostic tool (for individuals), and the Social Impact *Culture* Type diagnostic tool (for businesses). These are methods to uncover the ways you or your company find the most meaning and enjoyment in doing good. By learning about the different ways to do good and what about them resonates with you or a company as a whole, you (or your company) fall into one of three Types: Activator, Investor, or Connector. Just like with any personality type—there's no right or wrong! The idea is that you discover what works—and what doesn't—so you can focus on the right things and get, well, unstuck.

I met Laura when she was CEO of Crown Philanthropic Solutions, on the day I signed the papers to sell Embolden to Crown. We were co-presenting at a Council on Foundations conference in October 2014. The topic was donor engagement. With no time to prepare in person, we had relied on digital communication to gear up for the conference and pull together a professional focus to our meeting agenda! Digital had taken off in philanthropy as well as everywhere else, and we both loved testing ways technology could work harder to further the goals of nonprofits, businesses, and each one of us in doing good, or creating "social impact." When I learned about the Social Impact Personality/Culture Types, everything clicked for me. I really could have used that knowledge at Embolden!

FOREWORD

In getting to know Laura and her team's work, I realized how far they'd taken the idea. They knew that just like with any sort of discovery, understanding and naming it is really just the first step. They wanted to inspire people and companies to *use* their Type to build habits and programs and make the most of their "doing good." She was developing a Social Impact Platform service for companies to do just that, and she wondered whether I might like to help.

I didn't hesitate for a moment. I'd always believed in empowering people to do well by doing good. The Social Impact Platform is about giving people a tool so they can reach their potentials and maximize success. It's about giving people a boost. There is no greater thrill for me than building something that *actually works*. Something works when an organization or business gets more out of it than what it paid for it, whether that something is an Embolden website or, today, a Social Impact Platform.

As Laura and I continue to develop the Social Impact Platform, I think of my role as a leader at Embolden, and what I would have loved to have known about my team's Social Impact Personality Types and the resources I would have liked to have had to embolden my own company to do more good. I also think about today's talented professionals and their heightened desire to make a difference and be part of something larger than themselves. That's really important because fulfilling a company's mission for success begins with its people.

DO GOOD, *Feel Better*

So that's what this book is about—you. It's about realizing what truly gets you going when it comes to doing good and, equally as important, just how much good you're already doing. By learning about the different ways to do good and finding your Type, the good just grows—along with all the positive feelings that come with knowing you're changing the world, adding meaning, making a social impact, and building on your own success.

Ann-Marie Harrington
Providence, Rhode Island
October 30, 2016

Getting in Touch with Your Good Side

What grew into a years-long intensive research project began the way a lot of big ideas do—with a curiosity that wouldn't let go. At the time, I was the CEO of the Greater Kansas City Community Foundation, an organization that administers more than $2 billion in assets. I thought I was working on a project to figure out how to make charitable giving a little easier and a lot more fun. In my team's early research, we quickly learned a few facts:

- People enjoy giving to charities—it makes them feel good.

- People recognize and give to big charities, but they also donate to local organizations and causes that are meaningful for personal reasons.

- With annual household giving averaging $2,974, and total annual giving topping $373 billion in 2015 alone, according to *Giving USA*, supporting charities is an important part of American life.

We loved asking our interviewees this question: *What are your favorite causes, and why do you enjoy giving to these charities?*

As my team and I interviewed more and more people, we noticed something else. Something that felt big and important and, well, good. When people talked about giving, they relaxed. They became more upbeat. They leaned in. They kept on talking. They were proud, confident...emboldened even. And they were *happy*. They felt better!

Try this: Think about the last time you made a gift to your favorite cause. You're probably smiling right now just thinking about it.

At first glance, philanthropy and positive psychology appear to have very little in common. Philanthropy is a term generally associated with giving money to charities, doing good in the community, and creating social value. Positive psychology usually connotes an academic approach to emotional strengths and virtues that enable people to thrive.

But there is indeed a connection. After all, philanthropy, according to the classic dictionary definition, means a "love of humanity" in the sense of caring, nourishing, developing, and enhancing "what it is to be human" on both the benefactors' and beneficiaries' parts. The connection is right there.

What's more, the benefits aren't limited to your mood. After scouring websites, journals, blogs, articles, and more, we uncovered dozens of studies linking philanthropic behavior and improved physical health. Research suggests activities such as volunteering and giving can lead to a longer life, lower blood pressure, and better pain management.

The 10 Ways to Do Good Emerge

We were hooked on the well-documented positive effects of charitable giving and wanted to know more. We wanted to understand the experience of charitable giving from the broadest point of view possible to discover human behaviors and emotions that extended beyond the act of writing a check and into the well-rounded lives of the people we were interviewing.

So we asked: *"What are your favorite ways to do good for others?"*

Wow! Little did we know that question would wind up being the single most important factor in our multi-year research study involving thousands of interviews with executives, human resources professionals, community engagement experts, donors to charities, civic leaders, teachers, mothers, fathers, children, and just about anyone who would talk to us.

By changing the subject of the question from "giving" to "doing good," exactly *nine* more things happened.

But we're getting ahead of ourselves. First, many people wondered what "counted" as doing good; for example, did being on a school fundraising committee count if they weren't the head of it? Lots of people commented that they loved celebrating at charity events and thought that should count as making a difference. We heard about marketing favorite causes on Facebook. We heard about people cleaning out their closets and donating clothes to a homeless shelter.

We heard many, many good things.

We also heard one message loud and clear: *People are doing good in a variety of ways, and they want to feel even better about it.*

From the very first interview in our research, it was overwhelmingly clear that giving to charities was not the only philanthropic activity going on in the day-to-day lives of people like you and me. Giving turned out to be just one of ten "social impact" behaviors regularly practiced and enjoyed by the people in our study.

Through our hundreds of interviews and experiments in real-life situations, we observed and documented the contemporary point of view that philanthropy embraces the full range of social impact behaviors:

1. Caring about health and wellness

2. Giving to charities

3. Volunteering at a charity

4. Serving on a charity's board of directors

5. Purchasing products that support a cause

6. Recycling and respecting a sustainable environment

7. Donating items of food and clothing

8. Marketing a favorite charity

9. Sharing with family and friends in need

10. Celebrating at community events

We call these activities the "10 Ways to Do Good." We started out talking about one activity—giving—and it turned into more than three years exploring nine additional activities. One plus nine equals, you got it, the 10 Ways to Do Good.

People loved the 10 Ways to Do Good: They loved talking about them. When they did, they were happy and authentic and confident and empowered and full of optimism and possibility. We knew we were onto something.

So...What's Your Type?

The 10 Ways to Do Good were very good, but our curiosity wasn't satisfied. We'd noticed something else early on in our research, a pattern worth exploring, explained here in one of our early hypotheses:

Hypothesis: *Understanding our preferred social impact activities is the key to feeling even better about what we are doing to improve the lives of others.*

We coined this phenomenon "Social Impact Personality Type." Here's how it works.

Each of us has our own approach to "doing good." Each of us leans toward one of the three Social Impact Personality Types uncovered in our research: Investor, Activator, or Connector. Discovering your type will inspire you to focus on the social impact activities you enjoy the most. The result? You'll not only continue to improve the lives of others, but your own satisfaction will improve right along with it. You'll feel better about doing good. And who doesn't want that?

The Three Social Impact Personality Types: A Few Clues

- **Investors** prefer to engage in social impact activities that are independent and do not require scheduling dedicated time or working directly with others in the pursuit of a charitable endeavor.

- **Connectors** prefer to engage in social impact activities that are social in nature, involving the opportunity to get together with others.

- **Activators** are passionate about participating in the causes they care most about, and they tend to focus on "changing the world" and impacting one or more social issues on a broad scale.

INTRODUCTION

We've organized *Do Good, Feel Better* to help you get in touch with your Type through the social impact activities you prefer:

- Each of the following ten chapters gets you quickly up to speed on one of the 10 Ways to Do Good. A single activity is covered in each chapter. This activity will equip you with the background and vocabulary to be more comfortable with understanding and describing your own social impact activities.

- You'll discover which social impact activities you prefer over others. *You'll likely realize that you are doing more good than you thought.* You will also gain more confidence to give yourself permission to skip those activities that simply are not a good fit for you.

- Woven into each chapter are references to the points of view of each Social Impact Personality Type, so you can begin to figure out whether you lean toward Activator, Connector, or Investor. Look for these icons to signal when we're giving you insight into your Type:

And be sure to visit dogoodfeelbetter.com for even more tips on your Type!

- "Crash Courses" at the end of the book offer brief, easy-to-understand tutorials about social impact activities on topics you care about the most—success, lifestyle, community, money, and family. The series of articles will help you gain even more satisfaction out of doing good.

I hope by now you're already excited and feeling good about the possibilities that await you. So let's get started. Let's find out the best ways for you to feel good about doing good.

CHAPTER 1
Caring

Celebrating "what it is to be human" begins with *you*.

It started with a phone call in the summer of 2010.

I was sitting at my kitchen counter, talking on the phone with my sister. We were chatting about kids and birthday cakes, actually, and then the conversation turned to work. At the time, I was the CEO of the Greater Kansas City Community Foundation. I was working with our team on a project to make charitable giving easier, more fun, and more rewarding.

"Did you know," I asked my sister, "according to the classic dictionary definition, 'philanthropy' is 'a love of humanity in the sense of caring, nourishing, developing, and enhancing what it is to be human on both the benefactors' and beneficiaries' parts?'"

My sister is a psychologist. I am a lawyer. We are both entrepreneurs. We are always up for conversations that involve new discoveries.

I was a little embarrassed to admit to my sister that I was finally looking up "philanthropy" in the dictionary after more than a decade working in the charitable giving industry. Then again, things have a way of happening at exactly the right time. I doubt I would have caught the significance of the dictionary's words if I'd looked any earlier.

"So," I continued, "philanthropy—doing good for others—was always meant to have side benefits for the people doing the good, ever since the Greeks started using the term in the fifth century BC."

I'd been thinking about philanthropy, a lot. Yes, it was my job to interact with hundreds of families, individuals, and businesses engaged in charitable giving. But the main reason philanthropy was on my mind was because I had begun to notice that the way people were viewing "doing good" was changing, right before my eyes. Specifically, people were becoming more interested in pursuing philanthropy through social impact activities that made *them* feel good as well as making a difference in others' lives.

I wanted to know what my sister thought about this. "Do you suppose there is a link between philanthropy and positive psychology?" I asked.

"I think you are really onto something," said my sister. I could tell she was nodding on the other end of the phone, sitting at her kitchen counter in North Carolina. "Let's keep talking about this."

At that point, a child on her end of the phone needed help tying a shoe and a child on my end of the phone wanted more cereal. "We'll talk soon," we said to each other, and we hung up.

That's where the research began, at our kitchen counters, at the unexplored intersection between the disciplines of philanthropy and psychology.

And to say we kept talking is an understatement.

Fast forward. Six years later, after dozens of conversations with my sister, hundreds of interviews and surveys, and seven deep dives into the academic literature, the connection between psychology and philanthropy has stuck. Philanthropy—celebrating what it is to be human—starts with *you* and discovering the mix of social impact activities you enjoy.

Not long ago, "doing good" in the minds of many Americans meant giving to charities, volunteering, and sometimes serving on a nonprofit board of directors or committee. But with the rapid rise of social consciousness, philanthropy is expanding to cover far more territory than one or two ways to do good. And in the 10 Ways to Do Good that emerged from our research, *caring* was at the top of the list, part of everyone's Social Impact Personality Type.

Caring is important because humans are much better equipped to help others when they are also taking care of themselves. It's that simple.

> **"Caring" means acting on a commitment to your own physical and mental well-being.**

What is *caring* exactly? Whatever makes you feel good. Daily yoga might be something you are committed to doing to take care of yourself. Exercising, eating nutritiously, expressing gratitude, spending time with people you enjoy, acknowledging your self-worth, and taking time for self-expression through journaling or interacting with others are also examples of caring. Does that cup of coffee first thing in the morning start your day off right? Or do you look forward to your walk to the mailbox when you get home each afternoon? That counts. Caring means whatever activities you believe are important for your overall well-being. These, in turn, prepare you to help others improve their lives, too.

Caring as part of the 10 Ways to Do Good reflects a lifestyle in which social impact and wellness are intertwined. Does it surprise you to see caring listed as one of the 10 Ways to Do Good? The research surprised us a little bit, too, at first. But the theme was so pervasive in our studies that it was an easy decision to include it.

CARING AND THE THREE SOCIAL IMPACT PERSONALITY TYPES

Caring is the only one of the 10 Ways to Do Good that appears consistently across all three Social Impact Personality Types, with more than 95 percent of the participants in our research reporting that "caring" is part of their overall portfolio of social impact activities. That is because caring plays a big role in the way people view social impact as part of a well-rounded life. You can begin to see evidence of your own

Social Impact Personality Type through the lens of this vital way to do good.

Activator

What an Activator says about caring:

- "You have to be in touch with your own basic needs before you can truly help others achieve their own."

- "It is really important to my mental well-being to stay current on humanitarian events and the overall challenges of our society. This better equips me to make a difference and makes me feel educated on the issues."

- "My beliefs are part of my core. I believe people should have access to health care and healthy food—in developing countries, in our schools, and in my own home, too."

Four Caring Activities Activators Enjoy

1. Traveling on a mission trip over spring break to a location you've always wanted to visit.

2. Planting an organic garden with your favorite vegetables.

3. Gaining leadership experience for your career by serving on the neighborhood association board of directors.

4. Getting regular massages to build energy reserves.

Connector

What a Connector says about caring:

- "Treat yourself the way you would expect others to want to be treated."

- "We are all in this together, and each of us is worthy."

- "What goes around comes around."

Four Caring Activities Connectors Enjoy

1. Asking guests to give birthday gifts to your favorite charity in your name.

2. Recycling the soda cans from your frequent weekend gatherings.

3. Hosting a cocktail party to help a charity announce a capital campaign and also to enable you to network with guests.

4. Encouraging friends to join you in frequenting a charming coffee shop that supports a local scholarship fund.

Investor

What an Investor says about caring:

- "I can't do much good for other people if I am not in good shape myself—mentally, physically, financially."

- "It's like they tell you on every flight—put the oxygen mask on yourself before you assist those traveling with you."

- "If you can give a little, you have a lot."

Four Caring Activities Investors Enjoy

1. Taking a few minutes every morning to arrange your priorities for the day, including saying "no" to event

invitations that take you away from being most productive.

2. Planning your retirement and setting your financial goals high enough to live the lifestyle you desire and still have enough to give to charity.

3. Leading a social impact initiative in the workplace that drives bottom line results and also creates benefits for the community.

4. Returning glass bottles to the store in exchange for cash.

CARING + SOCIAL IMPACT "IN THE REAL WORLD"

Two examples from our research highlight what it looks like when caring and social impact intersect in our society. (Hint: It's good.)

Research Case Study

Finding "Someone to Save the World With"

"Neqtr is a relationship app for socially conscious people looking for love or friendship. We welcome people like you who believe in love, a healthier self, and a better world."

When a company describes itself on LinkedIn with words like that, you know "doing good" and "caring for yourself" have become more than just a couple of catchy phrases. They've become a way of life.

CARING

Just ask Sonya Davis, the founder and CEO of Neqtr.

"Social impact shows up in our dating culture and millennials' desire to do good," she said. "One of the big reasons I created Neqtr was because I wanted millennials to have a low barrier of entry to opportunities to give back and simultaneously connect with others who care about themselves as well as others."

And that's exactly how Neqtr works. You choose a common interest—rescuing stray animals for example—and Neqtr helps you make a date out of it. According to Sonya, "You shine your brightest when you're doing what you love. That's how we make giving back sexy."

Sonya has data to back it up, too. "Fifty-six percent of millennials are motivated to give back for the opportunity to meet people who care about the same causes and interests," she said. "And 94 percent of millennials who volunteered in the last year said it improved their mood."

When we met Sonya during our multi-year project to discover the elements that make up today's social impact footprint—the 10 Ways to Do Good—we decided "caring" should be at the top of the list. The notion that social impact works best when you're doing what you love was a theme repeated throughout the research study. And, as Sonya realized, it can feel downright amazing when you're doing *what* you love with *someone* you love.

Research Case Study

Location, Location, Social Impact?

"I want to live an active, healthy, well-rounded life, where connection to my community and my own well-being go hand in hand."

Which of the choices below describes the source of that statement?

A. Written response to a survey of people who work at nonprofit organizations

B. Quote from an interview with a candidate running for political office

C. Summary of the perspectives of target residents in a new housing development

D. Overheard while volunteering at a children's hospital

If you answered C, you are correct.

This statement originated as part of a market research study to determine the social impact lifestyle motivations of homebuyers and tenants. Our team analyzed recurring themes in hundreds of survey responses related to residential preferences and giving back to the community. The goal was to distill the social impact factors with the greatest influence when a socially-conscious person is making a choice about where to live, a key decision that reflects caring for yourself and your family.

Here are a few factors that respondents listed as important:

- Respecting the natural environment, especially focused on preserving trees and natural plant life

- Convenient recycling services and facilities

- Proximity to retailers with a track record of supporting local charities

- A community feel, including a published calendar of events and notifications about nearby fundraising events such as 5Ks and golf tournaments

- Periodic farmers' markets and access to organic vendors

- Trails and traffic patterns that accommodate running, biking, and walking

- Builders and subcontractors who can demonstrate a commitment to community organizations

- Opportunities for children to volunteer in the neighborhood for community service hours

What gives? Why do these things matter? Because *they make you feel good*. And they show that social impact lifestyle, or caring + social impact, is a very real thing.

A Few Good Thoughts

Doing good begins with you.

The "big data" uncovered in our literature reviews and during the interviews tells us that philanthropy has found a place in society's conversation about well-being. Little data tells us that, too. From the early days of my law practice, I observed that families who added charitable giving into their estate plans seemed to have better lives than those whose plans didn't include charitable giving. Their businesses grew faster. They had more money. They were more cheerful in meetings and more pleasant on the phone. They had nicer things to say about their children and their friends. They were healthier. They smiled more. The discovery of "caring" as one of the 10 Ways to Do Good helps explain why doing good so frequently translates to doing better.

Caring for your mental and physical health is the first step in doing the most good for others. Pay attention to what makes you feel better, and always remember to celebrate the little things. Philanthropy is about being human. That means you.

CHAPTER 2
Giving

Giving a little means you have a lot.

"What does your research say about gratitude?" I texted my sister. "I'm testing a few of my social impact theories with the kids."

I'd just cleaned up a full mug of hot chocolate that had spilled on the couch. (For the record, that full mug of hot chocolate was not supposed to be anywhere near the couch. And neither the hot chocolate nor the couch got close together on their own.) My plan was to clean up the hot chocolate, extract a thank you from a third grader, and then carefully observe her facial expressions to get a gratitude reading. I wanted to see exactly how being thankful made my daughter feel. My little girls were quickly becoming useful research subjects as I dug deeper into social impact behavior.

"Ah, yes," my sister texted back. "Definitely gratitude is a rising star in psychology circles." My sister checked the research files. "In a series of studies at the University of California, people categorized as 'grateful' reported feeling 25 percent more happiness and energy—and 20 percent less envy and resentment—than ungrateful people."

Bingo. I hit the call button. My sister answered her phone.

"Why do you want to know about gratitude when your research is about doing good?" my sister asked, sounding intrigued. "Isn't that a little twisted around?"

It was a good question. But I had been at this research project long enough to have a good answer. "I'm interested in the gratitude effect on the person giving to a charity. It's part of my theory that social impact activities actually make you feel better. I'm discovering that the benefits of philanthropy come full circle."

By then, I was deep into the research. I'd become convinced that giving to a charity is a powerful reminder that if you can give a little, you've got a lot. In my book, that's called gratitude. And gratitude was landing smack dab in the middle of the intersection between philanthropy and positive psychology.

The research on the benefits of gratitude is growing, my sister confirmed. People who practice gratitude report stronger immune systems, more positive emotions, lower blood pressure, increased happiness, more compassion, and fewer feelings of loneliness.

Practicing gratitude goes hand-in-hand with giving. Our 10 Ways to Do Good research suggests that feelings of gratitude are one of the most powerful benefits philanthropy can offer to the person doing good for others. Here's why: When you write a check to your favorite charity, or throw coins into a donation box, or support a cause through a donor-advised fund, your actions automatically reinforce that you've got something to give. You become more grateful for what you have.

And of course, "giving" is one of the 10 Ways to Do Good.

For lots of people, giving is a key component of their Social Impact Personality Type.

"Giving" means contributing money or stock to a charitable organization recognized by the IRS.

Let's take a closer look at giving in the context of social impact behavior. Giving under the 10 Ways to Do Good means contributing money to a charitable organization qualified under Internal Revenue Code Section 501(c)(3). Giving is important because the charitable organization, in turn, uses the money to support people in need, pay for educational and research activities, engage in the arts, or pursue other charitable endeavors.

What counts as *giving*? Giving includes writing checks, donating stock, making grants from a family foundation, or even dropping coins in a fountain to support a children's hospital. When you give, you are contributing to a charity that is improving the quality of life for others.

GOOD NEWS ABOUT GIVING

Pop Quiz! Which of the following statements is true?

A. Historically, charitable giving rises about one-third as fast as the stock market.

B. The majority of high net-worth donors give to charities to save taxes.

C. Most of the charitable dollars each year are given to support the arts.

D. Charitable giving is on the decline in America.

If you answered A, you are correct.

But something unusual is happening now…something *good*. According to *Giving USA*, Americans gave $373.25 billion in 2015, *reflecting a 4.1 percent jump from 2014.*

"Between 2010 and 2015, growth in charitable donations actually outperformed growth in GDP. Consider this: inflation-adjusted total giving grew at an annualized average rate of 3.6 percent during that time frame; meanwhile, GDP growth grew at an average rate of 2 percent," said Jeffrey D. Byrne in a press release. Byrne is the chair of The Giving Institute and president and CEO of Jeffrey D. Byrne + Associates in Kansas City, Missouri.

Bet that got your attention!

GIVING BY THE NUMBERS

Where charity dollars go

33%	religion
15%	education
12%	human services
11%	grant-making foundations
8%	health
7%	public/society benefit
5%	arts/culture/humanities
4%	international affairs
3%	environment/animals
2%	restricted gifts to individuals

The biggest area of increase

International affairs, which saw a 17.5 percent rise over 2014.

In total, 98.4 percent of high net-worth households give to charity…and nearly two out of three cite "giving back to the community" as a chief motivator.

— *Giving USA, 2015*

How 501(c)(3)s can spend their money

…according to the IRS (Internal Revenue Service):

> The exempt purposes set forth in Section 501(c)(3) are charitable, religious, educational, scientific, literary, testing for public safety, fostering national or international amateur sports competition, and preventing cruelty to children or animals. The term charitable is used in its generally accepted legal sense and includes relief of the poor, the distressed, or the underprivileged; advancement of religion; advancement of education or science; erecting or maintaining public buildings, monuments, or works; lessening the burdens of government; lessening neighborhood tensions; eliminating prejudice and discrimination; defending human and civil rights secured by law; and combating community deterioration and juvenile delinquency.

Remember, the tax rules are complicated, but giving doesn't have to be. Pick a charity you like. Give money. Know you've made a difference. Be grateful. Feel good.

GIVING AND SOCIAL IMPACT PERSONALITY TYPE

Giving is popular! It popped up in almost every social impact survey we conducted. The 10 Ways to Do Good would not be complete without it.

Still, giving is not for everyone. Some people don't have the financial means to give money to charities. Others prefer the hands-on involvement they get through a few of the other 10 Ways to Do Good. And some people like to incorporate social impact into their everyday activities, without any impact on their budgets.

If giving is in the mix of your own social impact activities, it's worth checking out how it might influence your Social Impact Culture Type. For example:

Activator

What an Activator says about giving:

- "I want to be sure the dollars I am giving are making a real difference. I want to see impact."

- "I always devote the majority of my annual giving budget to supporting charities that are working to solve large-scale social issues."

- "My giving dollars will make a bigger difference if I am personally involved in a charity's programs. That's the only way I can tell if my money is actually helping people in need."

Four Giving Activities Activators Enjoy

1. Giving an increasing amount of money each year to a favorite charity based on the organization's demonstrated results to improve the quality of life for the people or causes it serves.

2. Giving money to three different charities collaborating to achieve a specific goal, such as increasing the graduation rate within a particular school, discovering new drugs to treat cancer, or rebuilding a community center in a blighted neighborhood.

3. Giving to disaster-relief efforts after a hurricane, tornado, or earthquake.

4. Giving money to charities with the condition that the charity report back on the results achieved with the money (e.g., 100 meals were served to homebound seniors).

Connector

What a Connector says about giving:

- "You never know when you might be at a point in your life where you need help from a charity. It's important for people both to give to, and receive from, each other."

- "It makes my day to get a thank you note from a charity promptly after I send a check."

- "Some of my best friends are the people who work at the charities I support."

Four Giving Activities Connectors Enjoy

1. Hand-delivering checks to charities as an opportunity to say "hello" and "thank you" to the people working so hard to improve the lives of others.

2. Giving money to a best friend's favorite charity.

3. Collaborating with family members during the holidays to make one big gift to a single charity instead of many small gifts to different charities.

4. Encouraging children to add money to a piggy bank designated for charity and then mailing the money to the charity in an envelope with pictures drawn by the kids, or giving online with a credit card and emailing the pictures.

Investor

What an Investor says about giving:

- "I always check out a charity's financials before I write a check by going online to GuideStar and looking at the charity's Form 990."

- "Our family considers gifts to charity as part of our overall investment portfolio. We are investing back into the community that has allowed us to be so successful."

- "Maximizing the charitable deductions available under the Internal Revenue Code for giving to charity is the big win-win in philanthropy."

Four Giving Activities Investors Enjoy

1. Structuring an estate plan to include several bequests to favorite charities.

2. Giving appreciated stock to a charity instead of cash, to minimize capital gains tax exposure.

3. Setting up a donor-advised fund to organize annual giving to charities.

4. Establishing a budget at the beginning of the year to include a percentage of income designated for gifts to charity.

GIVING + SOCIAL IMPACT "IN THE REAL WORLD"

An example from our research paints a picture of giving as part of an overall social impact footprint in today's culture.

Research Case Study

Guilt-Free Giving

In 2011, the team at the Greater Kansas City Community Foundation conducted an experiment with a summer camp designed to explore what works best to ignite the spirit of generosity and charitable giving in young girls.

Each camp session—hosted in my basement!—featured an aspect of social impact, wrapped into a fun, age-appropriate format to connect social impact values to real life. (If you're wondering what in the world would keep a group of ten-year-old girls occupied for hours in a basement during the middle of the summer, keep in mind that cake played a major role in every session.)

Over the summer, the girls learned a lot about philanthropy, including how to research charities online, how to identify causes that meant the most to them personally, and where they'd like to give charitable dollars if they had them to spend.

What was the most important lesson *we* learned during the six-week study? It turned out to be pretty simple. When it comes to giving, positive reinforcement is a must. In particular, we discovered how important it is to reinforce that every gift to charity is good regardless of the profile of the giver, the size of the gift, or the charity receiving it.

We were particularly struck by what happened when we performed a simple role-play to test reactions during a mock dialogue about giving. The camp counselor kicked it off with a question: "What should you say when a friend tells you about the $25 check she wrote to her favorite charity?"

Next, girls were asked to read two different possible responses to the question and discuss the pros and cons of each:

Response A:

> "Wow! You gave $25? That is so great! Bet that felt good! How generous! I would love to hear more about your interest in helping that cause and what inspired you to make the gift."

Response B:

> "Well, $25 is okay, but gosh you could do more I am sure. And what did you give it to? Oh, *that* organization? Well, they are not that great. Let me help you make a better choice, assuming you are willing to write bigger checks."

Ouch! The girls cringed at the sound of Response B. Of course they did!

Response A encourages charitable giving. It is positive and upbeat. It makes giving feel good. Response B does the opposite. It conjures up feelings of guilt, inadequacy, and even regret.

Of course, conversations in real life are not as extreme as these examples. It's interesting, though, as the team noted in its research report on the results of the camp experiment, to observe the subtle messages that fill the giving space in our society, online, in our communities, among friends, family, charities, and even sometimes by the givers themselves.

In short, positive reinforcement plays an important role in your satisfaction with your own giving. Positive reinforcement is well-regarded as an effective motivator. It only makes sense that the principle would hold true in philanthropy, too.

Here's what my sister had to say when I told her about the camp experiment and asked her to jot down a few notes for my research files:

> Positive reinforcement is a powerful tool. Even in the most basic situations, adding a positive element to increase a response not only is more effective to motivate behavior, but it also prompts both parties to focus on the positive aspects of the situation. Punishment, when applied immediately following the negative behavior, can be effective, but punishment

can result in extinction of the behavior altogether and evoke other negative responses such as anger and resentment.

I told you my sister was smart!

Positive reinforcement in charitable giving is effective because it first engages the charitable giver's own understanding of what it means to be philanthropic—how much, to whom, and why. So remember, if giving is one of the ways you do good, you'll be a lot more satisfied with your experience if you listen to the positive voices around you and ignore those that make you feel inadequate or guilty.

A Few Good Thoughts

Give because you want to give.

Giving to charities is as American as wrapping paper and cheeseburgers. Still, just because you give money to a charity doesn't necessarily mean that you will see a benefit on your tax return. That's because the charitable giving deduction is currently available to taxpayers who itemize deductions rather than applying the standard deduction.

So let's wrap this up with an important reminder. A tax deduction can be a nice perk. But it isn't the reason you're doing good. As my tax professor in law school said, "You don't give away a dollar to save thirty cents."

GIVING

You're giving because giving is one of the ways you enjoy doing good for others. It's how you express your love of humanity. It fills you with gratitude. It's philanthropy, it's social impact, it's good for the community, and it's good for you, too.

CHAPTER 3
Volunteering

Roll up your sleeves for your favorite cause.

"Did you know," I asked my sister one morning in October, "that there are many ways to do good and be socially responsible without inviting a rodent to spend the weekend in your home?"

My sister laughed. "What are you talking about?"

"It's actually not funny, at least not right now," I said, taking my second Diet Coke of the morning out of the refrigerator. (And that was after my coffee run two hours earlier for a desperately needed latte.)

I explained to my sister that my daughter's second-grade teacher had asked for a volunteer to take care of the class pet, Furball, a hamster, for the weekend. I'd been feeling a little bad about not signing up to be a helper at the upcoming Halloween party, so in my weakened state of mother guilt, instead of asking myself, *Is this really a way you want to do good?*, I said "Yes" to the hamster visit.

Then 2 a.m. came, when I woke to a noise at the bedroom door. *Scratch, scratch, scratch. Scratch.* I poked my husband, who groggily but graciously flipped on the lights and opened the bedroom door. In a furry flash, Furball bolted through the open door like a cannonball, ran across the floor, and darted under our bed. Hamsters are fast! It took us ninety minutes, two brooms, one flashlight, and a complete rearrangement of furniture before we finally trapped the hamster between a wall, one of the brooms, and a chair. We locked the hamster in its cage, this time with duct tape slapped across the door.

Now my sister was really laughing. "That's not the worst of it," I said, laughing a bit myself. "This morning, I discovered that the hamster had not only scratched up the bedroom door, but also had eaten a whole section of carpet, redistributed the garbage from the trashcan, and munched half of a Halloween costume."

"I guess you won't be doing that volunteer job again," my sister remarked. "What did the kids say about it?"

"They said the hamster bit them three times. It was no fun to play with." Which was just as well because after the thorough duct-tape job, there was no way we were getting that hamster back out of its cage. Game over.

VOLUNTEERING

It's a good thing most volunteering experiences aren't anything like the hamster sleepover. Still, I always like sharing that story because it reinforces that volunteering comes in all shapes and sizes. One size does not fit all where social impact activities are concerned. And a miss or two doesn't mean you're just not cut out to volunteer. To that point, my sister brought up our first volunteering experience together:

"Remember when the company you worked for hosted a Saturday street party for all the kids enrolled in a local after-school program?" she asked. "They shut down a city block downtown and the employees spent Saturday playing games with the kids. For those kids, it was a full day of fun with caring adults and a rare experience in their lives."

I did indeed remember that day. "That was actually a double volunteer event," I reminded my sister. "I roped you into it with me. I volunteered to help at the event, and you volunteered to help me do it. Kind of like when we were little and I would volunteer you to help me clean out my closet."

"Right," she said. Then she added, "The day of games was more fun than the closet cleaning, though." It was more fun than hamster-chasing, too.

Think about the last time you volunteered for a favorite cause. If you're like most Americans, you enjoyed it! Indeed, volunteering is popular among the 10 Ways to Do Good, with an average of 73 percent of the people across our series of focus groups reporting that they volunteer at least once each year.

Examples of volunteering include serving meals in a soup kitchen, sorting clothes in a homeless shelter, helping out at a school, or picking up trash on the side of the road. According to the Bureau of Labor Statistics, a few of the most popular volunteering activities include tutoring, serving food, providing

> **"Volunteering" means a hands-on contribution of your time to an organized cause that helps others.**

transportation, coaching youth teams, offering management assistance, mentoring youth, helping out with office work, being an usher or a greeter, and performing music as a community service.

The Corporation for National & Community Service offers a wealth of information about the health benefits of volunteering. For example, research studies indicate that volunteering improves self-worth and feelings of accomplishment, as well as enhancing a person's social networks. These dynamics help decrease stress and reduce the risk of disease.

VOLUNTEERING BY THE NUMBERS

Americans contribute nearly *8 billion* hours of service annually, according to the Corporation for National & Community Service. In 2013, that figure represented 32.1 volunteer hours per person.

Top Ten States for Volunteering

In the United States, the rate of volunteering is highest in Utah, where an average of 46 percent of residents volunteer at least once each year. Wow! Here's how the Top Ten breaks down:

Utah	46.0%
Idaho	35.8%
Wisconsin	35.4%
Minnesota	35.3%
Kansas	35.1%
Vermont	34.7%
Nebraska	34.6%
Alaska	34.3%
South Dakota	34.1%
Iowa	33.0%

That's not all! The Corporation for National & Community Service keeps health and volunteering data from the U.S. Census Bureau and the Center for Disease Control. The data indicate that states with a high volunteer rate also have lower rates of mortality and incidences of heart disease. The data also show the reverse: Health problems are more prevalent in states where volunteer rates are lowest.

VOLUNTEERING AND SOCIAL IMPACT PERSONALITY TYPE

Volunteering can take many forms. Learn how Activators, Investors, and Connectors feel about it and incorporate it into their lives.

Activator

What an Activator says about volunteering:

- "I feel like the hands-on experience really gets me in touch with what my favorite charity is doing. When I am interacting with the people it serves, I know I am making a difference."

- "The best way to learn about a cause is to understand it from ground up."

- "When I am working side-by-side with the people who work at a charitable organization, I am showing the charity that I truly care about the cause. I am not just checking a box."

Four Volunteering Activities Activators Enjoy

1. Before committing to spending time with an organization, researching volunteer opportunities to be sure the experiences match favorite causes and personal goals for community impact.

2. Volunteering at three or four different organizations that support the same cause in order to attack a particular social problem from multiple angles.

3. Aligning volunteer activities to match specific professional skills.

4. Reflecting on each volunteer experience and asking oneself how his or her work connected directly to improving the quality of life of others.

Connector

What a Connector says about volunteering:

- "My personal, professional, and family relationships are greatly enhanced when we volunteer together."

- "Every volunteer event should include time to socialize and make friends with the people who work at the charitable organization."

- "I am always looking for recreational activities that involve an element of volunteering."

Four Volunteering Activities Connectors Enjoy

1. A weekend outing where a few hours are spent volunteering, followed by a social hour, group lunch, or hosting a dinner at a volunteer's home.

2. Regularly polling a group of friends to decide where to volunteer, and switching it up every month.

3. A volunteer opportunity that involves working one-on-one with the people and families served by a charitable organization.

4. Scheduling a volunteer event with children, parents, siblings, and cousins around the holidays as a way to bring the whole family together.

Investor

What an Investor says about volunteering:

- "I enjoy volunteering when I can sign up for a specific time, show up for an hour, and do something that I know can be completed during the time I am there."

- "I am happy to volunteer when the location is convenient, or when I am going to be there anyway."

- "Time is money, so I think of volunteering in terms of the opportunity cost of the time I am choosing to invest."

VOLUNTEERING

Four Volunteering Activities Investors Enjoy

1. Assisting with cleanup at the school carnival during a designated thirty-minute time block.

2. Dropping by over the lunch hour to assist the book-keeper at a charity that is located a few blocks away from the office.

3. Offering to drop off leftover flowers from the church service to a homebound member of the congregation who lives down the street.

4. Spending a few minutes each month helping edit a charity's email newsletter.

VOLUNTEERING + SOCIAL IMPACT "IN THE REAL WORLD"

Volunteering is a hot ticket in corporate America. A large majority—71 percent—of companies offer company-sponsored volunteer projects, and 60 percent give paid time off for volunteering, according to America's Charities. In many cases, volunteering works well for companies, employees, and the community. But it's not a fail-proof endeavor, as our next case study reveals.

Research Case Study

Beware of "Corporate Cram-Down"

In roughly one-third of our workplace focus groups, we discovered a bit of a sticky wicket...a phenomenon we coined the "corporate cram-down." The following example involving volunteering perfectly illustrates the issue:

An accounting firm had a longstanding history of community involvement and civic responsibility. So long, in fact, that it was a big part of the firm's brand and company values. As part of its community engagement program, a couple of times each year, the company hosted a Day of Service. All partners, associates, and staff were strongly encouraged—and in some years required—to spend eight hours rolling up their sleeves volunteering for a community cause. Sometimes, the day was spent rehabbing a house in a blighted neighborhood. Other times, employees stocked shelves at a local food pantry, picked up trash in urban neighborhoods, or fixed playground equipment.

No one questioned the worthwhile nature of the projects, yet all was not well in the world of corporate good. Why? *Because these volunteering activities were simply not the way most of the people at the accounting firm preferred to do good.* Other social impact activities were more in line with the firm's "Social Impact Culture Type"—the aggregate of employees' Social Impact Personality Types. How did we know? Only 23 percent of the participants in the focus group said that volunteering was one of their preferred 10 Ways to Do Good. By contrast, giving, recycling, and donating topped the list, with more than 90 percent of the firm's employees reporting that they enjoyed these activities the most.

Comments from employees reinforced this sentiment:

"I just don't feel like I can take a full day off of work to go do a volunteer project, when I am expected to bill a certain number of hours a year. Plus, I have young children, and getting away on a weekend for a Day of Service is really tough. But I'm happy to donate canned goods, or even write a check, to support the firm's overall community engagement effort."

"I'm really involved with the fundraisers at my church and at my kids' school. I feel like I do a lot of good in my personal life, and I'm not sure how I feel about my employer telling me how and when to give back to the community. It feels a little heavy-handed. I know the firm is trying to do something good, and I really appreciate that, but it seems easy for the message to become mixed and backfire."

As more companies recognize the rewards of doing good, the risk of "corporate cram-down" grows as well. Companies try to do the right thing by offering employees opportunities to get involved, but selecting activities that are not in line with employees' preferences results in, at best, an unsettling dissonance and, at worst, a community engagement program that does more harm than good to the company's culture. The formula to avoid this common error? Discover your workplace's Social Impact Culture Type—then match your community engagement program to it. It's simple but powerful.

A Few Good Thoughts

My parents went to Bermuda and all I got was this lousy T-shirt.

DO GOOD, *Feel Better*

Remember that slogan? Perhaps the most fun discovery we uncovered in our research about volunteering was the power of the T-shirt. For instance:

- "We all got together to fix up a house and we got to wear these really great T-shirts with our company logo. It was great for the photo op!"

- "Our department got T-shirts for our community service project. We came up with a name for our team, a logo, and a slogan, and then we ordered the T-shirts. It was really fun to wear them on the community service day and show our team and community spirit all at the same time."

- "I took the kids to volunteer at the animal shelter. The shelter gave each of the kids a T-shirt. The kids wear them all the time! I think it's because doing good is a cool thing to do and they are proud of the time they spent to make life better for others."

So how 'bout it? If volunteering is one of the ways you like to do good, dig up one of your favorite charity T-shirts and wear it proudly! Or volunteer to be in charge of ordering T-shirts for a service project near and dear to you…. They mean more than you know!

CHAPTER 4
Serving

Sometimes the people behind the scenes are the ones
making the biggest difference.

My first time serving as a director was a stint on the neighborhood homeowners' association board. Did that ever give
me a huge appreciation for people who take on that task!
I had no idea how much work went on behind the scenes
to manage things like collecting dues and setting a budget,
keeping the trash picked up, arranging for maintenance of
the pool and park, and communicating regularly with residents. Not to mention the occasional incident requiring the
board to enforce the rules with a homeowner who wanted to
pursue a remodeling project that fell outside the bounds of
the neighborhood's use restrictions. (Purple paint, anyone?)

Since then, I've served on a lot of boards, each with its own
colorful personality. Take the arts center, for instance, an ad-

venture early in my board service career. I was working late one evening at the law firm, finishing up a few estate planning documents for a client, when I heard someone walking down the hall.

A senior partner popped her head into my office. "Do you have a minute?"

"Of course!" I said. That was the only possible answer for me, a first-year associate.

"I am on the board of directors of a charitable organization that offers art classes and family services to kids in a very challenged part of town," she said. "One of the charity's long-time donors just died. We've had an interesting issue crop up with something she left to the charity in her will."

She had my attention! My job was to draft wills and trusts and then help administer estates after people passed away. This included preparing tax returns, filing probate papers, and transferring property to family members and other beneficiaries, including charities. *I'll bet I can help*, I thought to myself.

"Sounds interesting," I said. "What's going on?"

The partner explained that a woman who had supported the arts center for many years had died and left her largest asset to the charity. "The asset is a bit of a challenge," she said.

"What is it?" I asked. I was initially thinking along the lines of cash, stock, bonds, or real estate, and then my mind shifted to things like jewelry or artwork. I was going down a mental list of all the things you could give to a charity and ticking off the ones that might be a challenge. Maybe it was a coin collection, herd of cattle, or even a fancy car.

"It's a pipe organ," she said.

"A pipe organ?" I sunk a little lower in my chair behind my desk. I had a feeling this was not going to be easy.

"Yes, a pipe organ, and not a small one. A full-sized pipe organ, like the kind in churches and baseball stadiums. We think she might have been swindled into buying it. She practically spent her life savings on it. But the good news is that it does have some value if we can sell it. The board doesn't know what its options are in this situation."

Next thing I knew, I'd joined the board of directors of the arts center, initially to help with the pipe organ bequest. Dealing with the pipe organ required getting a valuation by a pipe organ expert, finding a buyer to convert it into cash, and fighting off claims from the music store owner that the woman still owed him money on the purchase price. After a couple of legal skirmishes, we finally got the charity its money. The lawyer for the music store was not exactly a charming character. Resolving the issue involved a few minor scratches and bruises. But it felt so good to know I'd helped someone support the charity she loved and saw that her wishes were carried out, even after she was gone.

That was the first and last bequest of a pipe organ I would ever deal with! It was not, however, the last charity board

I would serve on. Each board has taught me a lot about the inner workings of charitable organizations and the challenges they face carrying out their missions. And it's definitely taught me that without a doubt, serving is one of the 10 Ways to Do Good.

> **"Serving" means being active on a board of directors or similar group for a community or civic purpose.**

Three Key Jobs of a Board Member

If serving is part of your mix of social impact activities, it's a good idea to review periodically the responsibilities required of a charitable organization's director.

Here's a handy checklist of the three key responsibilities:

1. **Mission:** The board is in charge of making sure the organization is achieving measurable goals to carry out the charity's purpose. Charitable status carries with it a host of requirements under state corporate law, overseen by the attorney general, as well as tax laws set out in the Internal Revenue Code. In addition, the board is ultimately responsible for ensuring that the charity's programs are actually working.

2. **Leadership:** The person responsible for the day-to-day business of the charity is the executive director, chief executive officer, or a person in some other designated position charged with oversight of the

charity's operations and programs. The board's responsibility is to oversee this person, including hiring and firing the position. Additionally, the board has to govern itself and elect new members and officers according to its bylaws to make sure the governing body stays healthy and active.

3. **Money:** A big responsibility of directors is to ensure that the organization has the financial resources to carry out its mission. This responsibility includes compensating employees, covering overhead, and paying for the expenses of the programs that are delivering on the charity's mission. In addition, the board needs to be sure proper financial oversight is in place with all the right legal and accounting controls. Finally, most boards expect directors to give financial support in some form, whether that is in the form of personal gifts, gifts from the director's company, or through the director's own efforts to fundraise on behalf of the charity.

Fulfilling your responsibilities as a board member requires a big commitment of time. For instance, BoardSource reports that nearly half of all charity boards meet more than six times a year, and 75 percent of charities ask board members to participate in an annual retreat.

Not everyone is up for the fiduciary responsibility and time commitment of the director role. That's okay! There are other methods of serving the charities and causes you love. For example, serving on a committee or task force does not carry the same fiduciary responsibility that comes with serving as a director, although it's still a big commitment of time and effort.

Remember: Serving in any form makes a big difference in the success of any charity or community cause.

SERVING AND SOCIAL IMPACT CULTURE TYPE

Serving tells you a lot about your Social Impact Personality Type. People tend to be hot or cold on serving. Either you love it—or you don't. Check out the way serving plays out for each Social Impact Personality Type.

Activator

What an Activator says about serving:

- "Strong missions require strong stewardship. I feel a responsibility to be a part of sustaining a mission for many years to come."

- "Good governance is every bit as important in the non-profit sector as it is in the for-profit sector. Return on investment for the community is the payback for the dollars put into a charity."

- "If you are really serious about positive social change, you ought to serve on the board of at least one of the organizations that is dedicated to the larger cause you are pursuing."

Four Serving Activities Activators Enjoy

1. Chairing a board of directors.

2. Serving on a civic task force to explore options for re-developing blighted areas.

3. Joining a task force to generate support for a ballot initiative that would direct tax dollars to health care access.

4. Being part of the steering committee for a community needs assessment.

Connector

What a Connector says about serving:

- "Being on a board of directors is a great way to meet other leaders in the community."

- "I like getting involved in the PTO because I can stay

in close touch with the parents of my kids' friends."

- "Joining the fundraising task force was the most fun I've ever had with a charity event. Testing out caterers with the other people on the task force was great. We made an evening out of it, every time!"

Four Serving Activities Connectors Enjoy

1. Serving as a director of two or three (or more!) charities at a time.

2. Hosting the board of directors meetings at their home or office.

3. Never missing a board or committee meeting.

4. Signing up for the image and awareness task force for a brand new charity.

Investor

What an Investor says about serving:

- "When I get the pre-reading materials before each board meeting, I immediately flip to the financials and check the projections against budget."

- "As a board member, I expect to receive information demonstrating a direct link between the charity's work and an uptick in the quality of life of the people receiving services from the charity, measured in level of income, if possible."

- "As a board member, my responsibility includes writing a check each year to the charity, even if my budget permits only a modest gift."

Four Serving Activities Investors Enjoy

1. Joining the investment or finance committee of a charity's board of directors.

2. Setting up regular meetings or phone calls with the charity's executive director to get a ten-minute briefing on exactly where the charity stands against its goals.

3. Setting expectations with the other board members and the executive director that board meeting attendance might be sporadic, given other demands on time.

4. Researching a charity before agreeing to serve on its board to ensure that the charity is not the subject of lawsuits or bad press.

SERVING + SOCIAL IMPACT "IN THE REAL WORLD"

It can be really hard for a charity's leaders to find the right board members. According to a report issued by Board-

Source in January 2015, only 73 percent of chief executives at charities agree that they have the right board members. Furthermore, fewer than 20 percent of charity executives *strongly agree* that they have the right board members to oversee and govern their organization effectively.

Board service is a challenging job. We wanted to know why.

"What are the most important realities facing the boards of directors of charitable organizations today?"

Over the course of our research, we asked that question of every person we interviewed who was either currently serving on a charity's board of directors or had served as a director within the last twelve months.

Overwhelmingly, the most common answer was: "Fundraising, especially getting new donors involved."

We dug deeper.

Research Case Study

Four Steps to Finding New Donors

Nearly 1.5 million charitable organizations in America are doing everything they can to secure a share of the 2 percent of GDP representing annual philanthropy. Bringing new donors into the fold is the key to sustaining a mission for the long haul. Yet it's actually quite difficult to convince someone to get involved in a charity for the first time. In fact, based on the *Money for Good* studies, together with feedback from our hundreds of interviews, we estimate that 90 percent of donors will give where they want to give, even when presented with information about a different worthy cause that might achieve *an even greater impact* on the community.

Somehow, though, boards of directors and the teams they lead have to get inside the heads of today's donors. The future of charitable organizations depends on it. So how do you do it? Our deep dive into donor motivation offered a few clues. Through a series of three pilot studies, our team identified a four-step process that charities can use to drive new donor involvement. We call it "authentic social impact engagement."

Here's how it works:

1. **Affirmation:** Similar to positive reinforcement, "affirmation" means acknowledgment—without judgment—that the potential new donor is already doing a lot of good. For example, a charity will have much better luck engaging a new donor with a comment like: "You do so much in the community! Thank you for your commitment to philanthropy." Than this: "We'd love for your support to start flowing in our direction."

2. **Education:** A charity has to show the potential new donor what it's all about. Who else is on the board? What are the charity's programs and whom do they help? What are the quick facts about the charity's finances and history?

3. **Inspiration:** Stories are powerful. What's an example of a life that was changed for the better because of what this

charity does? How did support from donors help make that happen?

4. **Motivation:** A charity can offer a few simple ways to get involved one step at a time. For example, a board member could extend an offer to a prospective donor to take a tour, or ask a new donor for a modest gift to support an annual campaign. Or ask the donor to purchase a ticket to a fundraising event. Micro moves! Remember, people at all levels of giving frequently express this frustration: "I want to help, but I just don't know how I can help." It is not useful for a potential new donor to be told to "get involved" with nothing specific to back it up—no call to action.

A Few Good Thoughts

If you are serving, you are appreciated!

Serving is a terrific way to do good. But it isn't for everyone. Just for fun, take this quiz to see whether serving is for you.

Which of the following is your favorite way of serving the community?

A. Serving on a charity's board of directors.

B. Chairing a charity's board of directors.

C. Serving on the neighborhood association board.

D. Leading the committee for the school fundraiser.

E.   I really don't have a favorite! Serving was a bigger job than I expected.

If you chose E., that's okay! Serving is just one of the 10 Ways to Do Good, meaning there are nine other wonderful activities that might be more suited to your Social Impact Personality Type.

A final note of personal gratitude: Thank you to everyone who serves on boards of directors, committees, and task forces that strengthen charities and make our communities better. It is very hard work, requires a lot of time, and involves commitments that last months and even years. Serving often goes unnoticed, but it's what makes it all work.

CHAPTER 5

Purchasing

Change the way you think about shopping, for good.

If anyone tries to tell you that shopping and supporting a charity are mutually exclusive, don't believe it for a minute! You absolutely *can* support charities and shop at your favorite stores, all at the same time.

For three months during the social impact research study, we conducted a series of experiments involving kids, cakes, and charities. It went like this: During each session, we helped kids research charities online, explaining what the charities did to help make life better for others. The kids picked a charity to celebrate. Together, we then baked a couple of cakes and decorated them with a theme to showcase the charity's mission. From children's smiling faces to paw prints for homeless pets, each cake was unique, to say the least.

The last step in the experiment was to deliver the cakes to the charity or to someone who had been helped by the charity's mission. It was awesome!

Research charities. Bake cakes. Deliver cakes to celebrate. We repeated this process oh, say, about thirteen times. That's a lot of cake! But it worked. The whole point was to discover the principles that work best to teach children charitable values in real life. We learned that it's relatively simple to engage kids in social impact activities when it's fun and easy *and* when they get to pick the charities all by themselves.

I also learned how easy it is to do good while gearing up to do good. Let me explain....

One afternoon, I was stocking up on cake mix. I scanned the cake mixes in the baking aisle, doing a mental tally of how many cake mixes I'd need to buy to complete the experiments. I counted thirty. Thirty! *Here* goes, I thought, and I loaded up my cart with white cake mix, yellow cake mix, lemon cake mix, and various chocolate flavors of cake mix. German chocolate. Devil's food. Dark chocolate. Milk chocolate. (Did you know you can buy at least seven varieties of chocolate cake mix? Now you do!) Oh, and red velvet, too, a cousin of chocolate cake and a test kitchen favorite.

But I didn't grab just any kind of white or yellow or red velvet cake mix—I made sure to load up my cart with Betty Crocker. Why? Because Betty Crocker is a General Mills brand. Have you checked out General Mills lately? I have, and not just in the baking aisles.

PURCHASING

Here's what the General Mills website says:

> We have the greatest impact where our company's key strengths intersect with community needs. General Mills focuses our giving and volunteerism on:
>
> - increasing food and nutrition security
> - advancing agricultural and environmental sustainability
> - strengthening our hometown communities
>
> Our goal is to strengthen communities by increasing food security around the globe, while supporting the agricultural and environmental sustainability upon which our planet's food supply depends.

Fabulous!

And here's the icing on the cake:

> General Mills and our Foundation have given nearly US$2 billion to charitable causes worldwide since 1954.

Two billion dollars is some serious cash!

So what's this all about? It's about one of the 10 Ways to Do Good, called *purchasing*.

Have you ever bought a brand of pasta that supports food pantries across America? Do you feel good

"Purchasing" means buying products and services that include a charitable element.

when you know that a person across the world got a new pair of shoes, too, when you bought yours? If you answered "Yes," then purchasing is one of your 10 Ways to Do Good!

The Power of "Cause Marketing"

Let's get a better feel for purchasing in action with a Pop Quiz:

Massage Envy, Macy's, Best Buy, Vans, Staples, Bank of America, Ameriprise, Zappos, H&M, Samsung, Sprint, GameStop, Old Navy, and Humana. What do these companies have in common?

Here's a hint: The answer is related to these charities: Arthritis Foundation, Clothes4Souls, Americans for the Arts, DonorsChoose.org, Special Olympics, Feeding America, Best Friends Animal Society, DoSomething.org, Autism Speaks, and Boys & Girls Clubs of America.

If you guessed that these companies are the winners of the 2016 Halo Awards and the charities listed are the causes the companies supported, you are correct! (Your social impact IQ is off the charts, by the way.)

The Cause Marketing Halo Awards are North American cause marketing's highest honor. The awards are bestowed by the Cause Marketing Forum, Inc., a group founded in 2002 to increase successful company cause alliances.

You know a lot about cause marketing whether you realize it or not. That's because the idea has steadily become a powerful consumer dynamic ever since brands began aligning themselves with charities to benefit not only the brand but also society as a whole. Early cause marketing efforts included the Marriott's campaign with the March of Dimes in 1976, which was coordinated around the opening of a new hotel in San Diego, according to the Cause Marketing Forum. In 1979, Famous Amos Cookies launched a campaign with Literacy Volunteers of America, featuring Wally Amos as the spokesperson for increasing literacy rates across the country.

Since then, the techniques known as "cause-related marketing" and "cause marketing" continue to grow in popularity. The Cause Marketing Forum estimates that cause sponsorship will reach $2 billion in 2016, a 3.7 percent increase from 2015. In addition, 80 percent of global consumers agree that business *must* play a role in addressing societal issues.

PURCHASING AND THE SOCIAL IMPACT PERSONALITY TYPES

If you're like me and purchasing is one of your favorite social impact activities in the 10 Ways to Do Good, discover how purchasing plays into your Social Impact Personality Type with these insights about Activators, Investors, and Connectors.

Activator

What an Activator says about purchasing:

- "I pay attention to a company's story to figure out whether the company is for real. Does the company truly care about its people, its customers, and the community it serves? I want to know before I buy from it."

- "I need to know that there's really a 'cause' in the 'marketing,' meaning the charity actually benefits beyond just a few pennies and actual people are being helped."

- "I will consider switching brands if I happen not to believe in the specific cause a product is promoting."

Four Purchasing Activities Activators Enjoy

1. Paying attention to global supply chain standards and buying only those brands that have a true humanitarian focus.

2. Supporting brands that give back to specific causes in the local community.

3. Reading the fine print in the full description of the charity and how exactly it is supported by the brand.

4. Asking the executive director of a favorite charity for the names of merchants who support the charity's cause and then making a point to go to those stores.

Connector

What a Connector says about purchasing:

- "Brands that 'do good' are an important part of my personal and professional image. I wear them and use them proudly!"

- "When I have parties, I make a point to purchase beverages with a well-known connection to a charity displayed prominently on the label."

- "When my friends tell me about a store that's doing good in the community, I make a point to check it out."

Four Purchasing Activities Connectors Enjoy

1. Buying wrapping paper, candy, trash bags, and cookies from the kids who come to the door raising money for a school or athletic team.

2. Flipping through *People* magazine to figure out what cause-related brands celebrities are wearing.

3. Using trips to the grocery store with children as opportunities to educate kids about which brands give back.

4. Giving holiday gifts to friends and family purchased from stores that support a cause, and also including a note on the gift tag indicating the name of the charity supported by the purchase.

Investor

What an Investor says about purchasing:

- "Charities and businesses that work together through cause marketing are smart. They are leveraging consumers' desire to make a difference."

- "Contributing to a charity at the cash register of a retailer is awesome. So easy and efficient. Say yes. Swipe. Done!"

- "When there are two similarly-priced products, one from a brand that supports a cause and one that does not, I will always choose the cause-related brand over the brand that does not support a cause."

Four Purchasing Activities Investors Enjoy

1. Shopping at charity "stores" where the charity is running a retail operation to boost its income.

2. Making a note, mentally or in a notebook or a spreadsheet, of major purchases that supported a cause, and then counting an estimate of the charitable component of these purchases as part of an overall budget for social impact activities.

3. Wondering whether the price of a product is too high because the brand is supporting a charity.

4. Buying for true need rather than purchasing a product *only* because it supports a cause.

PURCHASING + SOCIAL IMPACT "IN THE REAL WORLD"

One of the most important factors related to purchasing as a social impact activity is women. Why? Because women tend to align their lifestyles with social impact activities to a greater degree than men. For instance, women are more likely than men to give to charity in the first place, and when they do give, they are likely to give more. They also do the majority of the purchasing. In fact, women influence or make 85 percent of all consumer purchases, according to Greenfield Online for Arnold's Women's Insight Team, and sh-economy. com. Check out how that breaks down in major consumer spending categories.

Women influence or make purchasing decisions for:

91% of new homes

66% of personal computers

92% of vacations

80% of healthcare

65% of new cars

89% of bank accounts

93% of food

93% of over-the-counter pharmaceuticals

And 100 percent of cake mix. (That wasn't in the research, but I'll bet it's close.)

To get a deeper sense of the issue, our team focused its research efforts on testing a 10 Ways to Do Good curriculum with women and kids. What could we learn about the emotional connections between the female consumer and her children on one hand, and social impact and consumer brands on the other?

Research Case Study

Color My World

To extract perceptions about the value of social impact in driving loyalty to a brand, we recruited thirty-four women in the Greater Kansas City area with one or more children under the age of eighteen. They were asked to complete a 10 Ways to Do Good drawing and painting exercise with their children designed to celebrate the good the families were already doing—regardless of the causes supported. Following the exercise, mothers were asked to participate in a brief online tutorial about the 10 Ways to Do Good.

PURCHASING

At the conclusion of the study, we asked three questions:

1. "If there were products on the market today that helped you engage with your family in one or more of the 10 Ways to Do Good, would you be likely to purchase those products?"

   85 percent answered YES, they would be likely to purchase those products.

2. "Are you likely to use part or all of the material in the survey to help teach your children or grandchildren, eighteen years of age or younger, about the 10 Ways to Do Good?"

   100 percent answered YES.

3. "Do you feel like you have a better mental picture of the day-to-day activities that are part of your overall social impact—how you are making a positive difference in the lives of other people?"

   91 percent answered YES.

Wow. With numbers like that, it only made sense to go deeper with sixty-minute individual interviews with participants. And the results were equally powerful.

- "I want a company to acknowledge my current situation as it relates to social impact."

- "I want a company to understand my need to educate my children about doing good."

- "I want a company to inspire me to involve my children in doing good."

- "I want a company to motivate me by making it easy for me to involve my children in doing good."

Color commentary was equally illuminating. Here were a few comments from the mothers in the study:

"I would purchase products that help me reinforce good values and morals with my daughter. I'm a single mom, so activities that are fun for her *and* let me spend a few minutes reinforcing our family values are very helpful."

— Marie, mother of a girl, age 8

"A company that can help me spend time with and interact with my family is a company I want to support."

— Christa, mother of one girl, age 5, and five boys, ages 7, 9, 10, 13, and 14

"I was surprised at how much good we are doing as a family. Sometimes you can get burned out doing the same things. The online survey reminded me that there are many ways my kids can be helpful and do good."

— Kate, mother of one boy, age 4, and one girl, age 8

PURCHASING

A Few Good Thoughts

Social impact goes beyond the shopping cart.

Most of the time, purchasing as part of the 10 Ways to Do Good involves buying consumer products. Don't forget, though, that purchasing as a social impact activity also includes buying services from companies that are giving back. It's worthwhile to ask or check out the websites of your bank, law firm, window washer, lawn service, insurance company, and health care providers to find out how they are making a difference in the community.

Purchasing goods and services to support a cause can be a fun and rewarding part of your portfolio of social impact activities. It's easy, too! Doing good is a piece of cake.

CHAPTER 6

Recycling

Loving the world we live in.

The look was unmistakable. Maybe I'd taken the social impact research a little too far.

My sister was visiting. My favorite times! She lives too far away. I miss seeing her, especially at moments like this, when I say something somewhat outrageous and she reacts with a combination of horror and amusement, but mostly amusement. I love that reaction.

"Tell me you did not go on television talking about the 100 percent recycled birthday party," she said.

"I think people liked it," I said enthusiastically, with maybe just a hint of defensiveness. After all, it was my job to figure out ways to celebrate philanthropy at home and in the workplace. It was all part of my master plan to help people turn all of their social impact activities into rewarding personal experiences.

"Did you at least leave off the part about using old tortilla chips from the pantry?" asked my sister.

"Nope!" I said cheerfully. Personally, I like the idea of arranging chips, pretzels, almonds, crackers, cereal, or whatever you find in your pantry on a beautiful platter and calling it birthday dinner. Or at least birthday brunch. "I also talked about using recycled wrapping paper, skipping the paper plates and napkins in favor of real dishes and silverware, and cutting up old birthday cards to make new ones." Plus using recycled ribbon. My mother taught me always to recycle the good ribbon. "See?" I explained. "It's the 100 percent recycled birthday party. Everything respects the environment. You can even have the party out on your lawn to save on indoor electricity."

My sister may have had a point that the 100 percent recycled birthday party was a little much for some people. Still, I wasn't sorry I had talked about the idea on the TV show. Inspiring people to get creative with social impact is what I'm all about.

I'm also all about serious ideas, too—my attorney and CEO side, I suppose—and learning about best practices toward social impact and sustainability, the *en vogue* term for recycling. Several years ago, I spoke with the head of Global Reporting Initiative (GRI), an international standards organization that helps businesses, governments, and other groups understand and communicate the impact of business on critical sustainability issues such as climate change, human rights, corruption, and many others. To me, GRI represents the commitment of hundreds of companies to strive toward a common set of benchmarks to protect the earth and humanity. More than 90 percent of the world's largest 250 companies are among the thousands of "GRI reporters," meaning they subscribe to the organization's standards for sustainability performance.

There's a lot to learn from efforts like GRI, which play a critical role in encouraging companies to report information that relates to "corporate social responsibility." Here are examples of the types of data points companies are encouraged to disclose to consumers, shareholders, and the public, beyond what's required by law:

- Efficient use of resources such as energy, water and land use, and materials
- Release of pollutants and greenhouse gases
- Production of hazardous waste
- Sourcing of materials and safeguards against trafficking
- Use of green products in production
- Respecting humanitarian issues and avoiding corruption

> **"Recycling" means furthering a sustainable and regenerative environment.**

On a small scale, at home and at work, activities include recycling bottles and cans and turning off lights. On a large scale, at multinational corporations, it can mean participating in corporate social responsibility initiatives like GRI reporting.

WHAT RECYCLING MEANS TO THE THREE SOCIAL IMPACT PERSONALITY TYPES

Recycling and respecting a sustainable environment are growing in popularity. Indeed, when we first began our 10 Ways to Do Good surveys in late 2012, an average of 82 percent of respondents answered "Yes," recycling is in the mix of their social impact activities. By early 2016, nearly 90 percent of most survey groups showed recycling as a preferred way to do good. Here is how recycling plays into all three Social Impact Personality Types.

Activator

What an Activator says about recycling:

- "It's our responsibility as humans and civilizations to leave the earth in better shape than we found it."

- "I make certain to track the latest scientific studies about global warming and the melting of the polar ice caps. I need to stay informed."

- "I simply cannot work for a company that does not clearly commit to best practices in sustainability."

Four Recycling Activities Activators Enjoy

1. Writing letters to elected officials advocating for conservation legislation.

2. Advocating for a zero-waste-to-landfill program at work.

3. Investigating best practices for a rooftop garden in the neighborhood and assisting with plans for its development.

4. Making phone calls to local food retailers who don't display recycling bins near the checkout counter or another spot where customers can easily deposit recyclable materials.

Connector

What a Connector says about recycling:

- "Our family loves spending time outside and appreciating the beauty of our natural environment."

- "I like to attend informational meetings in my community about the latest efforts to generate renewable energy."

- "My ideal workplace is a LEED certified building. The positive energy is a real boost for me and my colleagues."

Four Recycling Activities Connectors Enjoy

1. Structuring weekend outings around visiting a farmers' market.

2. Prioritizing national parks when selecting vacation destinations.

3. Adopting a family pet from rescue agencies or animal shelters.

4. Teaching children at a very young age about the rules for recycling.

Investor

RECYCLING

What an Investor says about recycling:

- "I don't hesitate to call my local waste management company whenever I have questions about how to get rid of large items, paint, and dead branches. I want to dispose of it in the right way."

- "We have a glass recycling center about a mile away, and I plan my route to work so I can drop off empty bottles."

- "Our neighborhood dry cleaners is environmentally savvy. The owner has won awards for its eco-friendly cleaning process. That's the dry cleaner I use!"

Four Recycling Activities Investors Enjoy

1. Growing organic gardens and using the produce at every meal possible.

2. Placing a recycling bin in every room of the house where waste is discarded.

3. Replacing plastic silverware with stainless steel (and volunteering to wash the dishes) in the breakroom at work.

4. Installing energy-saving light bulbs in every fixture in the house.

RECYCLING + SOCIAL IMPACT "IN THE REAL WORLD"

GRI and other corporate social responsibility reporting commitments make a lot of sense for many, usually large, companies. But in our research, we heard from companies who wanted to start with the basics and build from there. Many companies requested peer-to-peer education about social impact activities, information on corporate philanthropy, ideas for engaging employees in the community, and, in general, a better overall understanding of what "doing good" means for them. These companies were big enough for social impact to matter (every company!), but they were not a good fit for full-blown GRI reporting or a complex corporate social responsibility effort.

Our research team decided to fill this gap, creating the Social Impact Benchmark. Dozens of companies signed on to learn from us and each other, and to commit to making social impact an important part of their company's mission. Our team was super-impressed by the spirit of the group! Members hosted roundtables, shared ideas, and conducted workshops for each other. Intrigued? Visit socialimpactbenchmark.com to view videos of some of the sessions and learn more.

Not surprisingly, the members of the Social Impact Benchmark demonstrated leadership in many of the 10 Ways to Do Good, especially recycling and furthering a sustainable environment. Here is a snapshot.

RECYCLING

Research Case Study

Sustainable Vodka? Mmmmmm.

During the Social Impact Benchmark component of our research study, we were especially enamored with McCormick Distilling Co., Inc.'s commitment to the environment. Here's how we describe it in *Good. Celebrated.* magazine, which we published in late 2014 to recognize leading corporate social impact activities.

> At McCormick Distilling Co., Inc., being green is not a marketing gimmick, it's a way of life. Based on the principles of reduce, reuse, recycle, and rethink, McCormick created the world's first sustainable vodka, 360 Vodka. Everything about this Missouri-made eco-friendly brand is sustainable, from the recycled glass bottle to the paper used for the label to the ink and reusable cap. The vodka itself (let's not forget that!) features locally-grown grains distilled in an energy-efficient manner using a cutting-edge production process.

We asked McCormick Distilling Co. leaders to share how they incorporate the "4 Rs" in their vodka and tips for expanding the idea to everyday life:

Reduce

By sourcing everything for 360 Vodka within its home state of Missouri, the company reduces fossil fuel consumption in transporting raw materials to the distillery.

Everyday *tips for reducing:*

- Bring your own shopping bags to the grocery store to reduce plastic bag waste.

- Hang clothing to dry outside rather than using a dryer.

- Install flow-reducing shower heads, faucets, and other fixtures that reduce water consumption.

Reuse

The 360 Vodka bottle was entirely designed for reusability, thanks to the swing-top cap and bottle design. The company has seen consumers use it for water, olive oil, candies, and even wind chimes! Those consumers who don't wish to reuse their bottles can send the swing-top caps back to the distillery, in a prepaid envelope, where the caps will be cleaned and reused for the next 360 Vodka bottle.

Everyday *tips for reusing:*

- Carry a reusable coffee mug or water bottle with you during the day, rather than using disposable paper or plastic containers.

- Re-gift unused presents to avoid unnecessary waste.

- Reuse all bottles and jars of various shapes and

sizes to store items—just soak off the labels.

Recycle

The 360 Vodka bottle is made from 50 percent re-cycled glass and uses recycled paper on the label. Every year, the company recycles nearly 200 tons of glass, paper, and plastic materials, and manages the composting program for the largest cocktail festi-val in the United States, collecting more than 5,000 pounds of produce, which the company donates to a local farm.

Everyday *tips for recycling:*

- Buy products from environmentally-respon-sible companies that use recycled materials.

- Print documents on both sides of the paper and then recycle any unneeded pages.

Rethink

"Sometimes all it takes to help the environment is rethinking your usual habits," says Mike Harris, pres-ident of McCormick Distilling Co.

Everyday *tips for rethinking:*

- Plant a tree as a family activity or assist with a community cleanup project.

- Install fluorescent lights at home; they use 75 percent less energy than regular bulbs.

A Few Good Thoughts

Reflecting on your everyday activities is a source of social impact inspiration.

Making the environment a priority is a powerful way for individuals, families, and communities to participate in the 10 Ways to Do Good. And there are so many good ways to do it. Rethinking how to do regular, everyday things or family rituals is one of my favorites, *a la* the 100 percent recycled birthday party. My java-loving friend totes her favorite reusable coffee mug everywhere. She loves that it keeps her coffee hot and doesn't contribute to landfills. And she gets a "personal cup" discount at coffee shops, which is not just a ten-cent savings but validation that she's doing good, which makes her feel good and inspires her to want to do *more* good.

Whatever you do to recycle, the earth thanks you. Keep it up and enjoy!

CHAPTER 7

Donating

Find freedom and joy in passing it on.

"I forgot all about the clothing drive at work today," my friend told me over coffee. "In a rush to get out the door, I grabbed my toaster to donate."

"Wow!" I said. "Your toaster? That was really nice! Charities do need kitchen appliances."

"Well, I didn't know that, but I am glad to hear it. But actually it was a little selfish. The kids always burn their toast in the morning, and the smell lasts all day. It even sticks to my hair and clothes. I go to work smelling like burnt toast!"

I laughed. "Well, I guess it's better than smelling like bacon!" My friend nodded in agreement.

Getting rid of your annoying toaster. Is that another side benefit of doing good? Perhaps!

All kidding aside, donating items of canned goods, gently-used clothing, and basic necessities is a really important way to do good. Millions of people depend on it.

To get a sense for the number of people who need assistance with basics like food and clothing, consider that 47 million people were living in poverty in the United States in 2014, according to *Poverty USA* and the U.S. Census Bureau. That's 15 percent of the population, and it represents a 2.3 percent increase in the poverty rate from 2007 to 2014.

Growing poverty levels means donations are needed and appreciated 365 days a year!

"Donating" in the 10 Ways to Do Good means collecting items such as food, clothing, and oth-

> **"Donating" means collecting necessities for people in need.**

er basic necessities to provide to charitable organizations, which, in turn, distribute the items to people in need. Examples of donating in action include food and clothing drives at the office, and holiday adopt-a-family initiatives to collect gently-used books and toys and even brand new toys.

Which items do you most frequently donate to charity? Jeans? Electronics? Canned goods? We asked that question in the survey we developed for our website, dogoodfeelbetter. com, to help people like you get a quick snapshot of your Social Impact Personality Type. If you're in a rush to get out the door, what do you typically grab in a pinch, if not your toaster?

WHAT DONATING MEANS TO THE SOCIAL IMPACT PERSONALITY TYPES

Your Social Impact Personality Type determines a lot about how you incorporate donating under the 10 Ways to Do Good into your lifestyle. See what donating means to Activators, Connectors, and Investors.

Activator

What an Activator says about donating:

- "Donating is one of the best ways to mitigate excess consumption, which is such a big issue in our society."

- "Before I donate anything, I call the charity to be sure it actually needs it."

- "I am always impressed when a charity takes donated items and resells them to the public. It's revenue for the charity to fulfill its mission, and it cuts down on waste."

Four Donating Activities Activators Enjoy

1. Researching which types of canned foods are most needed to meet the nutritional needs of the people served by a charity.

2. Encouraging an employer to make donations of excess inventory.

3. Combining donating with other ways to do good, such as serving on a board or giving to a charity that supports a high priority cause.

4. Making sure donated clothing is in good shape, and even sending it to the dry cleaners or making small sewing repairs before passing it along to a charity.

Connector

What a Connector says about donating:

- "I can't imagine not having a decent pair of shoes or a winter coat. I love knowing that I have filled that need for someone else."

- "When my kids don't finish everything on their plates or order too much at a restaurant, I remind them that food is a luxury for many people in our country and around the world."

- "I'm usually the one who organizes the canned food drives for the office and our neighborhood."

Four Donating Activities Connectors Enjoy

1. Shopping for a whole family during the holidays through an adopt-a-family program.

2. Setting aside one day every year to go through the house with the kids and gather up items for donation.

3. Asking guests at a birthday or holiday party to bring an item of nonperishable food to donate to charity.

4. Displaying the thank you notes from charities and the families they serve on the kitchen bulletin board for inspiration.

Investor

What an Investor says about donating:

- "Donating is really efficient. You can give the organization exactly what it needs—no administrative friction."

- "Companies that donate extra inventory to the charities are supporting the community effectively."

- "Sometimes the only things a family needs to get back on its feet are a few basic necessities like food and clothing."

Four Donating Activities Investors Enjoy

1. Estimating the value of donated canned goods and clothing and tracking it for tax purposes.

2. Going online to the websites of favorite charities and donating things from the "wish list."

3. Taking advantage of sales of nonperishable items at the grocery store to stock up on items to donate at a later time.

4. Keeping a box of used clothing in the closet at all times and, when it's full, taking it to a nearby shelter or donation box.

DONATING + SOCIAL IMPACT "IN THE REAL WORLD"

Social Impact in Action

A Neighborhood Food Drive Makes Donating Fun

Donating necessities is one of the 10 Ways to Do Good that kids love the most. The hands-on experience is a terrific way to help kids learn about the needs in the community. You can explain that many people don't have enough food to put on the table to feed their families, and then show kids how donations of canned goods help close that gap.

Here's a simple formula for food drive success:

First, share a few compelling statistics with your kids. According to the United States Department of Agriculture (USDA), 13.1 million children under the age of eighteen in the United States do not regularly get enough nutritious food necessary for a healthy life. This is called "food insecurity." When you're with your kids, pull out a map and review these facts from the USDA:

- Mississippi and New Mexico had the highest rates of children in households without consistent access to food in 2014, with 27 percent of the children in those states considered food insecure.

- By contrast, in 2014, the top five states with the lowest rate of food-insecure children under eighteen years of age were North Dakota, Massachusetts, Minnesota, New Hampshire, and Virginia.

Next, put together an instructions sheet, something like this:

Ann (11), Lindy (8), and Eva (5) are doing *socially-responsible* activities all summer for FUN! Helping others truly is fun, and you can help, too!

The girls are collecting items to take to The Robert and Shirley Meneilly Center for Mission on 99th and Mission Road next Wednesday, July 17th. After they drop off the items, they are going to tour the facility to see exactly how things are taken into inventory and then distributed to help families in need. Take time this weekend to shop for non-perishable items. See below for a suggestive list of items that the pantry is most in need of. You can leave this bag on your front porch on Monday, July 15th at 1:00 p.m. They will be walking around to pick up the bags. Any donation, big or small, is much appreciated and will help someone in need.

* If you have questions, please contact the Barker girls at 913-555-5555.

Suggested Items:
Canned vegetables, canned fruit, protein items (soups, canned Tuna, peanut butter, macaroni and cheese, one dish meals, etc.), pasta, cereal, sugar, flour, bread, buns, rolls, dairy products, fresh produce, dessert bakery items, frozen meats, personal items (toilet paper, toothpaste, feminine products, hand and body soap), household items (laundry detergent, dishwasher soap, etc.), and snack items.

Next, have the kids leave paper bags, with the instructions attached, on doorsteps in your neighborhood. Be sure to include the date you'll swing back by the front porches to pick up the bags. Then take all of the bags to the food pantry.

Finally, don't forget to pick up the bags on the day you say you will! Lonely bags sitting on porches, as cute as they may be, can't exactly walk themselves to the food pantry.

Research Case Study

A Cautionary Tale about Your Wardrobe

"I've got nothing to wear."

Who hasn't said that before? I used to say it a lot. But deep down, I knew it wasn't true. I'll bet I used to wear only 20 percent of the clothes in my closet. That's the percentage the average person wears on a daily basis, according to the chief design officer for California Closets quoted in *The Wall Street Journal*.

Then I started researching the social impact of simplifying my wardrobe. I learned lots from my friend, Barbara Fishman, owner of Savvy Style. She's a style consultant with a flair for both fashion and doing good. From a young age, Barbara learned about sewing through 4-H projects in her small town. She later spent more than twenty-five years working in psychology and nursing. Voila! The net-net is that Barbara has a deep understanding of both fashion and human behavior.

Barbara helped me cut back my closet to a fraction of its former self. I must have donated ten bags of clothes and shoes to charities! But donating wasn't the only good that came from downsizing. Barbara has helped me understand that today's "fast fashion" trend is creating a lot of challenges for communities and people around the globe.

Let's look more closely at the issue.

More than 80 billion pieces of clothing are purchased worldwide each year. That is a 400 percent increase from a decade ago! Those are the staggering statistics from *True Cost*, a 2015 documentary film about the garment industry. *True Cost* examines the global fashion ecosystem, from production and its impact on low-wage workers in developing countries to the environmental impact of the clothes we throw away.

A recent article in the *Atlantic*, "Where Does Discarded Clothing Go," offered these data points:

- In New York City alone, clothing and textiles account for more than 6 percent of all garbage, which translates to 193,000 tons tossed annually.

- Americans recycle or donate only 15 percent of their used clothing, and the rest—about 10.5 million tons a year—goes into landfills.

- Only half of donated clothing gets worn again.

  The good news here, though, is that much of the portion of donated clothing that actually can be recycled is ground down and re-formed into things like insulation, carpet padding, and industrial rags.

Reviewing your wardrobe with a critical eye and doing good go hand-in-hand. I've sure felt a lot better about my own social impact by paying closer attention to what I choose to buy. And when I stop loving that top or pair of jeans, I make sure to donate it to a charity instead of throwing it in the trash.

Don't forget that your clothing donations may be eligible for a tax deduction. The Internal Revenue Service requires that a value be placed on each item. So how do you know what it's worth? Check out Goodwill Industry International's suggested valuation of commonly donated items of women's clothing.

Tops, shirts, and blouses	$2–12
Sweaters	$5–15
T-shirts	$1–6
Dresses	$2–10
Skirts	$2–12
Jeans	$4–21
Evening wear	$10–30
Suits	$5–30
Robes	$2–10
Tennis shoes	$4–9
Sandals	$4–9
Ankle boots	$6–18
Handbags	$3–9

While you're at it, don't forget about household items, which also make excellent donations (even toasters).

Lamps	$4–12
Coffee makers	$4–15
Baking pans	$1–3
Coffee tables	$10–12
Desks	$30–60
Quilts/bedspreads	$8–24
Blankets/afghans	$2–15
Golf clubs	$2–25
Hardcover books	$1–3
DVDs	$2–5

A Few Good Thoughts

Donate outside of the box.

We've focused on donating clothes and food, but don't forget that other items make great donations, too. Many charities accept donations of cars, large appliances, building materials, office furniture, computers, and electronics. Some charities are even happy to swing by curbside at your house or come to your office to pick up things.

Last, but absolutely not least, if you're healthy and up to it, consider donating blood. Nearly 5 million people need a blood transfusion each year, according to the American Red Cross. When you donate blood, you are truly saving lives.

CHAPTER 8

Marketing

Like it. Love it. Tell everyone about it.

What would happen if you followed this recipe in your own kitchen?

> 1 cup of butter, or substitute
>
> 1 cup of sugar
>
> 2 tablespoons of milk
>
> 2 eggs
>
> 1 teaspoon of vanilla
>
> 2 cups of flour
>
> 2 teaspoons of baking powder

Cream butter and sugar; add well-beaten eggs, then milk, vanilla flavoring, flour, and baking powder. Roll thin and bake in quick oven (375°). Sprinkle sugar on top.

You'd bake up a batch of six or seven dozen of the original Girl Scout Cookies! Yep, that's right. And as Girl Scout Cookies approach their 100th birthday, it's hard to imagine a more successful marketing campaign for a charity.

The first Girl Scout Cookies were baked in 1917 in the kitchens of Girl Scouts in Muskogee, Oklahoma. The girls sold the cookies to fund their troop's projects. The cookies quickly grew in popularity as the idea spread to other Girl Scout troops. Babe Ruth even promoted the "Million Cookie Drive" during the 1924 World Series.

Annual revenue from sales of Girl Scout Cookies has consistently reached $700 million per year since 1999, according to a 2012 article in *Business Insider*. That's 200 million boxes of cookies—and a lot of money to the Girl Scouts, too: only 25 percent of the revenue goes to the bakeries, with nearly all the remaining going to support local Girl Scouts.

America's Favorite Cookie

If you guessed that Thin Mints are the most popular Girl Scout cookie, you'd be correct! Sales of Thin Mints average $175 million per year. The runner-up is Samoas (also called Caramel deLites). Yum.

MARKETING

How do the Girl Scouts do it? Read on for three reasons their campaign is so successful (and if you're into marketing, try applying these principles to promote *your* favorite cause).

1. **It's simple and fun.** People love to rally around initiatives they understand. Buy cookies. Support the Girl Scouts' mission. It's a win-win.

2. **Networks are powerful.** The Girl Scouts rapidly increased cookie sales in the 1920s and 1930s by tapping into the Girl Scouts troop network. With hundreds of troops across the country selling the cookies, the message about the Girl Scouts spread quickly. And to think that was before social media and the Internet! Even the telephone was still a relatively new invention.

3. **Celebrity endorsements go a long way.** In 1924, it didn't get much bigger than Babe Ruth as your spokesperson. Today, celebrities who actively promote their favorite causes include Leonardo DiCaprio, Mariska Hargitay, Brad Pitt, Angelina Jolie, Matt Damon, Bette Midler, Eva Longoria, Hugh Jackman, Emma Watson, and many more.

Whether you are Babe Ruth, who promoted Girl Scout Cookies, Matt Damon, who founded the charity that is now water. org, or just you supporting your own favorite charity, using your influence to spread the word about a cause really works. That's why marketing is one of the 10 Ways to Do Good.

> **"Marketing" means promoting a cause to encourage other people to support it.**

"Marketing" means anything you do to tell your family and friends about a favorite cause. This includes posting information on Facebook or texting a suggestion to support a charity. You might also enjoy telling your workplace colleagues about a favorite cause, whether that's recruiting people to fill a table at a gala or passing the Girl Scout Cookie order form around the office.

MARKETING AND SOCIAL IMPACT PERSONALITY TYPE

Your Social Impact Personality Type is a powerful influence over the way you take on marketing under the 10 Ways to Do Good. Here is what marketing looks like for all three types.

Activator

What an Activator says about marketing:

- "In my opinion, if you aren't willing to advocate publicly for the cause you love, you should really reconsider whether to get involved."

- "I am very focused on the overall network of the charities I support and how they reinforce each other. Those are the messages I share with family and friends."

- "I have connections with the media, and I use them to raise awareness about the causes that mean the most to me."

Four Marketing Activities Activators Enjoy

1. Writing letters to potential donors, encouraging them to support a cause.

2. Helping pay for and publicize a research study to identify the community's most urgent needs.

3. Assisting a favorite charity with communications strategies for demonstrating measurable success with the charity's programs.

4. Giving presentations about the importance of a favorite cause.

Connector

What a Connector says about marketing:

- "As soon as I hear about a fundraising campaign for my favorite charity, I post something on my Facebook page."

- "My kids and I all did the ALS Ice Bucket Challenge. Now that was having fun while 'doing good'!"

- "I always post information about upcoming charity 5Ks and golf tournaments on the break room bulletin board at the office. I also put up posters in coffee shops."

Four Marketing Activities Connectors Enjoy

1. Sending a big batch of emails to friends and families to help a charity meet a fundraising goal.

2. Regularly wearing T-shirts from charity sporting events.

3. Making phone calls to help fill a table at a charity gala.

4. Liking the social media posts and pages of every favorite charity.

Investor

What an Investor says about marketing:

- "It takes money to make money in business, and the

same is true for charities. Charities need to have at least a modest marketing budget to be able to sustain their missions."

- "I look for charities that have added a marketing professional to their boards of directors. This means they not only gain professional oversight, but they also might have access to pro bono assistance."

- "A charity's website must clearly indicate how a donor can give money online."

Four Marketing Activities Investors Enjoy

1. Paying for a favorite charity to get professional marketing assistance.

2. Writing content for a favorite charity's website.

3. Giving a charity a list of names for it to contact about an upcoming event.

4. Forwarding examples to a favorite charity of effective marketing campaigns going on at other charities.

MARKETING + SOCIAL IMPACT "IN THE REAL WORLD"

Research Case Study

How a Humanitarian Tragedy Changed Social Impact Marketing Forever

DO GOOD, *Feel Better*

On Tuesday, January 12, 2010, a major earthquake occurred sixteen miles west of Port-au-Prince, the capital of Haiti. Registering at a magnitude of 7.0, the quake and its many aftershocks caused catastrophic damage. The estimated death toll surpassed 100,000, and more than 3 million people were affected, according to authorities.

What does the 2010 earthquake in Haiti have to do with marketing and the 10 Ways to Do Good? This was the *first time* social networks played a major role in philanthropy. Accelerated by Internet connections and social media, millions of people got the message that relief organizations needed help. Individual donors contributed an estimated $43 million to the assistance and reconstruction efforts using the text messaging feature on their cell phones, according to a study conducted at the Pew Research Center. Fueled by the speed of communication, within days of the earthquake, more $200 million had been given to the relief effort. Within a year, total gifts and pledges surpassed $5 billion.

What's going on here?

Something new—and good. Analysts at the Pew Research Center, who studied the phenomenon, describe the "Text to Haiti" effect as "a new mode of engagement" that "offers opportunities to philanthropies and charitable groups for reaching new donors under new circumstances as messages spread virally through friend networks."

You've undoubtedly seen the "Donate Now" buttons on the websites of your favorite charities. You're probably also seeing opportunities to support a cause pop up across your social media accounts. It's easy to use your mobile phone to make a gift to charity when a particular cause or organization catches your eye and pulls at your heartstrings. This is known as "impulse giving." It's your instant reaction to the messages and images in front of you at that moment.

The 2010 Haiti earthquake caused impulse giving to go mainstream. According to the Pew research project:

- 89 percent of the people in the study heard about the "Text to Haiti" effort on television.

- 50 percent made their contribution immediately upon learning about the campaign.

- An additional 23 percent donated on the same day they heard about it.

- 75 percent of the Haiti text donors in the research said that their text message contributions typically result from spur-of-the-moment decisions.

That's not all. The message traveled! Forty-three percent of the Haiti text donors encouraged their friends or family members to make a similar contribution using their mobile phones, and nearly 75 percent of those they asked actually did make the gift.

What does the "Text to Haiti" effect tell us about marketing a favorite cause as part of the 10 Ways to Do Good? By studying the Pew research and conducting our own experiments using social media and online platforms to promote various causes throughout our research, we can draw three conclusions:

1. **Relationships tip the scales.** The single most important factor in impulse giving is who's asking. If it's someone you know and trust, you're much more likely to support the cause. That's partly because you inherently transfer the positive feelings you have about the person asking to the cause he or she is advocating, and you feel good giving without needing to take the usual time to research the cause. Is a good friend requesting the support? A well-respected member of the community? A celebrity? A friend of a friend? It matters.

2. **"Retail giving" = marketing.** The average size of an online charity gift is between $130 and $150, according to Blackbaud, a nonprofit technology solutions firm. Not bad! But what's really powerful about these gifts, especially from first-time donors, is that online engagement is often the first step for a charity to cultivate longer-term relationships with donors. So the charity not only captures the gift itself, but also gains an opportunity to build a future relationship with the donor—assuming the charity requests the donor's contact information and implements an intentional marketing plan to grow the relationship.

3. **The fewer the clicks, the better.** It's easy simply to follow a message and a link from a credible online source that takes you to a donation page. Ideally, you

won't need to take the extra step of finding one of the hundreds of donation platforms online and then selecting the charity. It's all about the fewest number of steps! Plus, these days, most charities' websites feature an online donation button to make it simple for donors to click and make a gift.

Online Giving by the Numbers

People love giving online! The M+R 2015 Benchmark Study of eighty-four charities, measured from 2013 to 2014, found that:

- Online giving increased 13 percent

- Website traffic for nonprofit websites rose 11 percent

- Monthly online giving grew 32 percent

- One-time online giving grew 9 percent

With online giving steadily rising, more and more charities are seeking gifts through their websites and social media. What's more, they rely on people who believe in their causes to use their networks to help them stand out in the crowd.

A Few Good Thoughts

Marketing is a key factor in the next generation's support of charitable causes.

A final note about millennials, the generation that is often at the center of the discussion of social media and the "connection economy." The Millennial Impact Report, conducted by the Achieve research agency and the Case Foundation, indicates that a whopping 65 percent of millennials are likely to volunteer if a coworker participates in a charity. Peer-to-peer marketing is *powerful*. The report also showed that only 11 percent give to charity through a payroll deduction. For years, the payroll deduction method of giving was the workplace standard.

Technology has made it easier than ever to encourage your friends and family to support a favorite cause. We won't be at all surprised to see the "millennial mindset" catch on across all generations as marketing continues to increase as a favorite among the 10 Ways to Do Good.

CHAPTER 9

Sharing

The original philanthropy, or "love of humanity."

There's a scene that repeats itself over and over at my house. The item in question has changed over the years, but the play-by-play is still the same.

It goes something like this: Child #1 yanks a Barbie sticker book right out of Child #2's hands. Catching Child #1 in the act, I jump into the fray. "What do we know about sharing?" I typically ask. "I don't like it!" retorts Child #1. This is followed by my futile attempt to convince my daughter that she shouldn't even want the book in the first place because all of the stickers are gone. But that would be too logical!

Sharing did not come naturally to my children when they were toddlers! As my girls get older, though, they are learning a lot more about the value of sharing. Not only does it keep them out of trouble, but they are learning that it also feels good to let others in on the fun of whatever you're doing.

Sharing isn't just for kids. Think about how many times each year or month you help out a friend, neighbor, or family member by giving a little bit of what you have. You might cook dinner for a neighbor who is under the weather, slip a few dollar bills into the envelope going around the office for a colleague who needs help paying medical bills, or stop by a retirement home with your kids during the holidays to drop off sugar cookies.

Sharing is part of the 10 Ways to Do Good because it captures philanthropic behavior that doesn't quite fit the Internal Revenue Code's definition of "doing good."

Here's a great example. A few years ago, a bank manager called me for legal advice. He was interested in collecting money to set aside for a ten-year-old's education. The child's parents, customers of the bank, had recently died in a car accident. The man wanted to do something good to help the little boy who was tragically left without parents.

"I'd love to set up a bank account and ask my friends at the office to contribute money to support the child's future education," he explained. "We've also had calls from bank customers offering to help. Is this something I can do?"

"Of course you can do that," I said. "What a wonderful idea!"

"Great," said the bank manager. "And we all will get a tax deduction for our contributions, won't we?"

Ooh. That's not how it works. "Unfortunately not," I said. I explained that the IRS does not allow charitable deductions for gifts that are intended to benefit specific individuals or families directly. "The issue is potential self-dealing and private benefit,'" I said. "There's no objective criteria or application process for selecting this child as the beneficiary," I explained. "For a charitable tax deduction to apply, you would need to set up the scholarship fund under a 501(c)(3) organization and then create an open process where this child and other children could submit applications for the funds. You would need an independent group of people to evaluate the applications, and there could be no guarantee that any particular child would receive the money."

"That doesn't make any sense," the bank manager said. "I'm not getting any benefit by doing this, and neither are the people who would be contributing money. But still no tax deduction. Are you sure that's right?"

I was sure. This is a question I hear a lot, actually, because so many people want to support friends and family in need. Many people assume there will be a tax deduction available for their contributions.

"It really is a nice thing to do," I said reassuringly. "Just because the IRS doesn't think it qualifies as a charitable contribution doesn't mean it isn't good. You are making a huge difference in the life of this child!"

The bottom line is this: You can't claim a tax deduction for money you give to friends, family, or other people in need.

But it's still "doing good"! Under the 10 Ways to Do Good, we call this *sharing*. Sharing means helping people directly in ways that don't fall under giving to a 501(c)(3) organization or otherwise qualify for a charitable tax deduction under the Internal Revenue Code.

Adding money to a medical fund for a specific coworker or preparing a meal for a home-bound neighbor are two examples of sharing as a social impact activity.

> **"Sharing" means helping one particular person, family, or group of people you select.**

In many ways, sharing was the original philanthropy, before the Internal Revenue Code defined charitable giving for tax deduction purposes. The income tax charitable deduction was first introduced by the War Revenue Act of 1917. At the same time, federal income tax rates were increased to help fund World War I. Lawmakers were worried that the increases in taxes would reduce support for charities, thereby increasing charities' reliance on government, which in turn would require another tax increase.

Love of Humanity

Philanthropy is a lot older than 1917! "Philanthropia" is a word from the ancient Greeks that means "love of humanity." For centuries, human beings have depended on kindness to each other. Interestingly, acts of philanthropy have not always been considered equal. More than 900 years ago, the biblical scholar Maimonides developed a hierarchy of philanthropic activities, rating activities on an ascending scale. At the low end are gifts made "reluctantly," or "grudgingly." At the high end of the scale are gifts that help others become self-supporting.

Check out Maimonides' list below.

1. One who gives grudgingly, reluctantly, or with regret.

2. One who gives less than he should, but gives graciously.

3. One who gives what he should, but only after he is asked.

4. One who gives before he is asked.

5. One who gives without knowing to whom he gives, although the recipient knows the donor's identity.

6. One who gives without making known his identity.

7. One who gives without knowing to whom he gives; neither does the recipient know from whom he receives.

8. One who helps another to support himself by a gift, or a loan, or by finding employment for him, thus helping him to become self-supporting.

In many ways, sharing is the "doing good original." A classic social impact activity!

WHAT SHARING MEANS TO THE THREE SOCIAL IMPACT CULTURE TYPES

Where would you fall on Maimonides' scale? Your self-assessment will give you a lot of insight into your Social Impact Personality Type. Read on for each Type's point-of-view on this early scholar's list:

1. One who gives grudgingly, reluctantly, or with regret.

Activator: "Regretting a gift is a shame."
Investor: "Your fault for making the gift in the first place."
Connector: "It happens sometimes…but just don't tell the recipient!"

2. One who gives less than he should, but gives graciously.

Activator: "Give what it takes to make a difference, whether you do it graciously or not."
Investor: "Giving in any amount is perfectly fine."
Connector: "The way you deliver the gift is even more important than the gift itself."

3. One who gives what he should, but only after he is asked.

Activator: "You should know the needs and not have to wait to be asked."
Investor: "Absolutely, you should be asked for your support. It's just like sales."
Connector: "I am honored when charities ask me to give."

4. One who gives before he is asked.

Activator: "Now you're talking!"
Investor: "Wait to be asked to let supply and demand work its magic."
Connector: "Everyone loves a surprise gift!"

5. One who gives without knowing to whom he gives, although the recipient knows the donor's identity.

Activator: "It is best to be sure you are giving where there is the greatest need."
Investor: "It does not make sense not to know where you are giving."
Connector: "I will find out who got the gift from the thank you note."

6. One who gives without making known his identity.

Activator: "Anonymous giving is an inspiration to people in need."
Investor: "That works."
Connector: "Ooh. That's a tough one."

7. One who gives without knowing to whom he gives; neither does the recipient know from whom he receives.

Activator: "This does not make sense to me."
Investor: "This does not make sense to me."
Connector: "This does not make sense to me."

8. One who helps another to support himself by a gift, or a loan, or by finding employment for him, thus helping him to become self-supporting.

Activator: "This strategy rocks!"
Investor: "This plan rocks!"
Connector: "This person rocks!"

A Few Good Thoughts

It all counts.

In many ways, sharing is about not leaving anything out. Caregiving is a terrific example. According to the Bureau of Labor Statistics, there are more than 40 million unpaid caregivers in America who are taking care of adults age 65 and older. All but 10 percent of these caregivers are helping an aging relative.

Many social impact activities, including caregiving, do not "count" as charitable contributions—according to the IRS. But they count immensely in the minds and hearts of the recipients and certainly show a "love of humanity." So sharing is definitely one of the 10 Ways to Do Good.

And speaking of not being left out, let's not forget sharing as it relates to some of our very important fellow earth inhabitants—animals! Taking your neighbors' dog for a walk while they're out of town—that's sharing with your neighbor and the pooch as well (plus caring for your wellness, another of the 10 Ways to Do Good).

CHAPTER 10

Celebrating

Every minute is a gift.

"Who was it who said, 'Showing up is 80 percent of suc-cess'?" I texted my sister one Sunday morning. I was out on a walk and thinking about social impact. I was still obsessed, but I was beginning to see a light at the end of the tunnel. I was finishing up the research on celebrating, the last of the 10 Ways to Do Good.

My sister texted back. "Ha! I thought it was 90 percent." My sister Googled it. "Can't tell the original source," she wrote. Versions of the quote are attributed to Woody Allen, Richard Rodgers, and even Thomas Edison. And my sister was right. Sometimes it shows up as 80 percent and other times 90 percent. Still, it's a lot!

I have always liked that quote. I think it applies to social impact activities. The point is, when you make an effort to be present with the people and causes you care about, good things happen.

Originally, our team included "celebrating" in the 10 Ways to Do Good because we wanted to capture the popular social impact activity of attending auctions, galas, 5Ks, golf tournaments, awards dinners, and other special events hosted by charities to raise money for their operations and programs.

Celebrating in the 10 Ways to Do Good means supporting favorite causes by showing up in person. People love celebrating social impact in their lives, work, and community. For example, employees frequently represent their companies at community events such as 5Ks, galas, auctions, and golf tournaments.

> **"Celebrating" means supporting favorite causes by showing up at events.**

Showing up at events is one of the 10 Ways to Do Good that has changed a lot for me over the years. My event attendance routine has included everything from going to formal evening galas and speaking at organizations' annual meetings, to taking the whole family out to a Saturday afternoon Walk for Williams Syndrome to celebrate our daughter with special needs and help raise money for the cause. Nowadays, we host a lot of informal dinners around our kitchen counter and spend time talking casually with the kids and extended family about the charities we support. At the moment, the last option is my favorite, although that could change!

CELEBRATING

Even in companies, sometimes the best celebrations are the informal gatherings, like the impromptu parties in the company break room to honor a colleague's birthday or favorite charity.

Attending events is an important part of celebrating, but it is bigger than that. Merriam-Webster defines *celebrating* like this:

1. To do something special or enjoyable for an important event, occasion, holiday, etc.

2. To praise (someone or something).

3. To say that (someone or something) is great or important.

Celebrating can apply to all of life's events, big and small, that are enriching and significant.

My sister knows a lot about this. She has her Ph.D. in psychology, and she is the founder of the Center for Mindful Development, PLLC. On her website, she defines mindfulness like this:

> Mindfulness is, at its essence, being fully present. It is being present in a way that is open, attentive, non-judgmental, and aware.

The way I see it, celebrating the causes you care about and reflecting on your favorite ways to make a difference in others' lives requires you to be mindful. It's how the 10 Ways to Do Good come full circle, from caring about your own health and wellness, all the way to celebrating the good you are already doing. Celebrating feels good. It makes you feel better about who you are and what you do.

PARTY TIME!

By now, you no doubt have a pretty good handle on the factors influencing your Social Impact Personality Type. You probably also have a new appreciation for all of the ways you are making a difference in the lives of other people through your social impact activities. You are doing a lot of good. Now it's your turn to celebrate!

Take a few minutes to jot down all the ways you do good on a blank sheet of paper, numbered 1-10. You can list the 10 Ways to Do Good in whatever order you like.

Here's an example of a checklist we created for one of our workshops:

10 Ways to Do Good

1 Giving money to a charity of choice, directly or through a foundation, whether it's tossing coins into a fountain or putting dollars in an envelope or writing checks or transferring shares of stock

2 Volunteering in the community or at your children's school . . . which, of course, includes visiting homeless puppies

3 Recycling and respecting a sustainable environment, even if it means just turning off lights and recycling your Diet Coke cans

4 Serving on civic boards and committees, whether it's the committee for the school fundraiser or the neighborhood association

5 Celebrating your favorite causes by supporting and attending community events, buying the occasional ticket to a charity event

6 Marketing with a focus on a charitable cause . . . maybe you've added your favorite causes to your Facebook page!

7 Purchasing products and services that include a charitable element

8 Donating inventory, or collecting necessities to give to people in need, such as canned goods or used clothing

9 Sharing with others, like your relatives, neighbors, and fellow employees, including preparing a meal for a family in need

10 Caring for your own health, keeping your commitment to wellness and physical fitness, gratitude, self-worth and self-expression

How You Do Good

Giving _____

Volunteering _____

Recycling _____

Serving _____

Celebrating _____

Marketing _____

Purchasing _____

Donating _____

Sharing _____

Caring _____

But it doesn't have to be that formal. You can jot down your Ways to Do Good just about anywhere—on your phone, on the back of your to-do list, or on whatever scraps of paper you find in your desk drawer.

Here is an example of a list created by a workshop participant in late December.

---

10 Ways to Do Good During the Holidays

Giving. While we were checking out cookie recipes online, we checked out a few charities, too. We Googled the kids' favorite causes by using key words like "children in need" and "homeless pets."

Volunteering. We delivered holiday cookies to the staff at a nursing home.

Recycling. We made sure to deliver our holiday treats to neighbors in reusable containers instead of using plastic wrap. I took the time to explain to my children why that is important.

Serving. I was on the committee to plan the kids' holiday parties at school. I told the kids that this was an important gift!

Celebrating. I showed my company spirit by attending the office holiday party where everyone donated canned goods and winter coats for a homeless shelter.

Marketing. I posted the office party photos on my Facebook page (well, some of them), and I included a shout out to the charity we all supported.

Purchasing. I took the kids shopping for holiday gifts and helped them spot all the opportunities to give back as we bought gifts for others.

Donating. See above. The office party checked two good boxes!

Sharing. We baked gingerbread cookies and decorated them with the names of the people our family loves. Then we delivered the cookies in person.

Caring. I had the kids make a list of the things they are grateful for, just before they made their lists for Santa. It boosted their moods, and mine, too!

Look at all that good! Make your own list now, tomorrow, and whenever you want to feel better. You are doing a lot more good than you know—so know it!

CELEBRATE YOUR SOCIAL IMPACT PERSONALITY TYPE

Think you know your Type? Here's what each Social Impact Personality Type might say about celebrating.

Activator

"I love the feeling of knowing I have made a difference. That's what's on my mind when I am running the 5K to honor my favorite charity."

Connector

"When I am with other people who support my favorite cause, I am energized. I know I belong."

Investor

"The charities I support are so smart about their special events. They raise money and awareness, efficiently. I am proud to support the cause."

CELEBRATING + SOCIAL IMPACT "IN THE REAL WORLD"

Big events are a big part of celebrating causes.

An organization called the Peer-to-Peer Professional Forum (formerly the Run Walk Ride Fundraising Council) does a great job tracking data and trends to support professionals who manage peer-to-peer fundraising events. Check out the Forum's Top Ten National Fundraising events and the dollars each raised in 2015!

American Cancer Society	Relay For Life	$308,000,000
American Heart Association	Heart Walk	$117,100,000
March of Dimes	March for Babies	$92,300,000
Susan G. Komen for the Cure	Komen Race for the Cure Series	$86,440,436
National MS Society	Bike MS	$79,969,124
American Heart Association	American Heart Association Youth Programs	$78,965,000
Alzheimer's Association	Walk to End Alzheimer's	$77,464,687
JDRF	JDRF One Walk	$70,459,004
American Cancer Society	Making Strides Against Breast Cancer	$66,300,000
The Leukemia & Lymphoma Society	Light the Night Walk	$61,176,000

That's a lot of money. But what's interesting is that according to the Forum's report, four of these ten events actually raised less money in 2015 than they did nearly ten years ago. The American Cancer Society's Relay for Life, Leukemia & Lymphoma Society's Team in Training, March of Dimes' March for Babies, and Susan G. Komen for the Cure's Komen 3-Day walk together raised $455.8 million in 2015. That's $254.5 million less than they raised in 2006!

That's still a lot of money. But it illustrates how things are changing in the practice known as "peer-to-peer fundraising." Peer-to-peer fundraising means that a charity's supporters are directly involved in the fundraising event by asking their friends, family, and workplace colleagues to support their participation in the run, walk, or bike ride by making a gift to the charity. Big events like these are powerful because they combine celebrating with giving and marketing.

According to the Forum, while a few of the larger campaigns have struggled, dozens of smaller events are gaining traction quickly. The way people enjoy celebrating their favorite causes is changing, right along with the increase in Americans' community-mindedness and social consciousness. For example, the American Foundation for Suicide Prevention saw more than an 18 percent increase in revenues between 2014 and 2015 through its Out of the Darkness Community Walks.

The key is to get creative with multimedia, tap into supporters' networks, and have a lot of fun. One of my favorite examples is the Big Slick Celebrity Weekend, now heading into its eighth year in Kansas City. The two-day series of events raises money for the Cancer Center at Children's Mercy Hospital. The idea is this: Hometown stars like Jason Sudeikis, Rob Riggle, and Paul Rudd join other celebrities in hosting events like a softball game at the baseball stadium, bowling, and an auction. Many events are open to the public, including 2015's red carpet arrival at the bowling alley. Tickets are sold to other events to raise money. Celebrity hosts also spend time at the children's hospital visiting cancer patients. The event engages audiences online by encouraging the public to vote for their favorite host. One dollar gets you one vote. Limited edition T-shirts are also available to support the cause. The Big Slick truly offers something for everyone. Now that's celebrating!

Here's an important point: Celebrating through events is valuable to a charity not only because it helps the charity raise money for its mission, but also because it helps the charity raise awareness and recruit new supporters. Charities are sometimes questioned about the "net revenue" earned for their missions through events after the event expenses are accounted for and paid. Fiscal responsibility is important, of course, and well-run charity events watch the budget closely so the margin stays in the black. But dollars raised is not the only measure of success. Charities can show a tremendous return on the investment of time and money spent on an event if they set—and meet—specific goals for building new donor relationships and strengthening existing connections.

A Few Good Thoughts

Blow out the candles.

Next time a birthday rolls around, instead of making just one wish before you blow out the candles, make two. One for yourself, and another for someone else.

Taking the time to think about other people is what doing good is all about. And it should make *you* happy, too. That's the big takeaway from our years spent gathering data, performing dozens of focus groups, and scouring the literature about philanthropy. When you are in touch with your Social Impact Personality Type, you'll naturally be drawn to the ways you find the most meaning and enjoyment in doing good. By learning about the 10 Ways to Do Good—caring, celebrating, and everything in between—you're sure to discover what it is about each of them that resonates with you.

Are you an Activator, Investor, or Connector? Take our Social Impact Personality Type quiz at dogoodfeelbetter.com and discover which one might fit you best. You can't go wrong! Philanthropy is about celebrating what it is to be human. What matters is that you feel good about the ways you're making a difference in others' lives and enriching your own life, too.

You are human. That's all it takes to make your life better.

Making Social Impact "Work" at Work

As you were reading *Do Good, Feel Better*, perhaps you became more aware of how your and your workplace colleagues' Social Impact Personality Types might roll together into an aggregate Social Impact Culture Type at your company.

Just like individuals, each workplace has a unique approach to doing good. Company cultures lean toward Investor, Connector, or Activator. Sometimes, a company falls between two of the types. For example, in our research, we discovered workplace cultures that we categorized as "Investor/Connector" and "Connector/Activator." We even encountered a few of the rare "Activator/Investor" cultures!

Why does Social Impact Culture Type matter in the workplace? It's important because today's market leaders view social impact behavior as a catalyst for building emotional loyalty with employees and consumers and, in turn, boosting business results.

The data points we gathered over the course of our research are validating:

- In his book, *Grow*, Jim Stengel, Procter & Gamble's former global marketing officer, released the results of a ten-year study of 50,000 brands. It found that a business built upon ideals outperforms the S&P 500 by four times.

- Deloitte's third annual Millennial Survey of nearly 7,800 Millennials indicated that a clear majority of the younger talent base wants to work for companies that are committed to charitable giving, volunteering, and making a positive impact on the bottom line and beyond.

- The 2014 Millennial Impact Study by the Case Foundation showed that 94 percent of people in this demographic want to use their talents for doing good.

- Working to benefit a good cause increases productivity by up to 30 percent, according to a 2015 study published in *Management Science*. While personal financial incentives have long been part of corporate culture, the study shows that social incentives such as gifts to charities also boost performance. Interestingly, the greatest increase in productivity was among those workers who initially fell into the "least productive" category.

Successful business leaders know social impact means success. Here's how it's described by the CEO of a financial firm in which every one of its 200 employees is involved in the company's community engagement program:

> We are proud of our culture of giving back. We know it makes us better as individuals and as a company. We talk about it all the time. It is a big part of the way we empower our team to achieve success. Social impact is a win-win proposition. We want to celebrate even more, because in this way we can grow from the experience and inspire other companies to follow our lead. Everyone succeeds—the employees, the company, the community.

Many Names, One (Big) Meaning

Companies use a variety of terms to describe social impact activities: Community relations, civic engagement, corporate giving, corporate citizenship, corporate philanthropy, corporate social responsibility (CSR), community investment, community engagement. Whatever words a company uses, the reality of today's workplace is that employees are doing good in many ways: Giving to charity, recycling, volunteering, serving on boards, donating canned goods or clothing, attending community events, marketing a favorite nonprofit, sharing with friends and families in need, purchasing brands that support causes, and caring for their own health and wellness.

Corporate Giving by the Numbers

Corporate giving in 2015 increased to $18.46 billion, representing a 3.9 percent increase from 2014.

— *Giving USA*

The Elephants in the Room

What do you think amazed us the most when we dug into the corporate phase of our research? We encountered two Reality Checks and one Massive Obstacle inside more than 85 percent of the companies we studied.

> **Reality Check:** Talented professionals want "doing good" to be a big part of the workplace environment.

> **Reality Check:** Market pressures on executives are mounting! Listening to the demands on corporate America to "do good" is like playing a game of lingo bingo: regulatory influences, sustainability trends, consumer preferences, corporate governance standards, philanthropic solicitations, and expectations of employees and recruits. It adds up to one big "What do we do?"

Massive Obstacle: Companies struggle when they try to make their social impact programs meet stakeholder expectations for community engagement and *also* support business goals!

We Had to Fix It!

We could not walk away from the research project and leave the elephants in the room. The Massive Obstacle was a loose end. A dangling participle. A missing punch line. It was making us crazy, just like the frustrated leaders inside the companies we studied.

So our team got busy. For months, we devoted every extra minute to developing a simple solution to help companies discover their Social Impact Culture Type. We call it the Social Impact Culture Roadmap. It's part of a set of tools called the Social Impact Platform that are designed to celebrate employees and gather valuable workplace data.

The Social Impact Platform started out as not much more than markers on a whiteboard. Check out a few of the things we jotted down as important elements of the final product.

Social Impact Platform Key Benefits Brainstorm

Features

- Online and in the cloud (means no work to maintain the survey function)

- Easy to use and deploy (and fun)

- Gather valuable data on the ten ways employees do good with real case examples of how they do good within each of the ten categories (e.g., number of hours volunteered, types of charities supported, charity events attended)

- The survey is the action; companies do not need to change their programs. All they need to do is celebrate.

Usefulness

Use the aggregate data to celebrate, engage, sell, market, recruit, and keep employees happy, engaged, and productive. Examples:

- **Recruit:** Include metrics on employee recruitment materials in print and online.

- **Retain:** Create an infographic poster of all the ways employees do good and hang it and/or post it on the employee intranet or next to the coffee machine in the office kitchen.

- **Engage:** Tweak community engagement programs to match Social Impact Culture Type that will engage the employee base, such as volunteering and mentoring programs, com-

> munity engagement staffing and programs, executive philanthropy programs, and decision frameworks for which charities to support.
>
> - **Sell:** Include social impact activity data in the survey in responses to RFPs and bids that require data points on employee engagement and community involvement.
>
> - **Market:** Tweet and create Facebook posts celebrating key data points that resonate with clients and customers.

"Oh, No! Not Another Survey!"

Wait! This one is different!

The Social Impact Culture Roadmap is not the survey tool you thought you knew! That's because we built the diagnostic after years of testing and getting feedback from hundreds of people who are responsible for community engagement programs and employee culture at their companies.

Why is the Social Impact Culture Roadmap a breakthrough tool for workplace engagement?

Three reasons:

1. The survey makes employees feel good about where they

work. Across the board—regardless of industry, geography, and size of company—participants loved the tech-savvy survey exercise. More than 97 percent of all respondents said the survey made them realize they were doing more good than they thought.

Here are examples of what people told us:

- "The survey made me feel validated for all of the ways I am helping out in the community. I can't always afford to give money, and I liked the opportunity to affirm for myself that I am giving back in lots of other ways."

- "I was really impressed that my company took the time to do this survey. It only took me ten minutes to fill out online, but still, it sent a clear message to me that I am working for a company that cares about me as a human being."

2. **The company gets a return on its investment**. In addition to the soft dollars that come from a boost in employee morale, companies benefit from the power of the survey data. Through the anonymous responses, the company's executives gain helpful insights into how employees like to do good, both at home and in the workplace. This allows company leaders to tweak their community engagement programs to match better with what employees actually enjoy.

Here are three examples of comments we heard from executives, human resources leaders, and community engagement professionals:

- "We found out that our employees really aren't using our matching gifts program, and would rather do something else. This allowed us to redirect the dollars from our budget to something more productive."

- "The survey data from the Social Impact Culture Roadmap showed us that 95 percent of our workforce was donating items of clothing and canned goods to people in need, at least once a year. We started using this statistic as a selling point in our recruiting materials. The 'doing good' part of our culture was the factor that tipped the scales with two key recruits who have now joined our team."

- "We discovered that our Social Impact Culture Type thrived through social events. So the committee in charge of our charitable giving started looking for opportunities to combine gifts to charities with opportunities for our team to get together in the community, outside of work, at galas or golf tournaments."

3. **Social Impact Culture Type rocks!** We already knew Social Impact Personality Type was a home run. Our focus groups loved it! The real test was whether the aggregate data—Social Impact Culture Type—would be a useful indicator in the workplace to create efficiencies and increase employee engagement.

The result? Thumbs up for the Social Impact Culture Roadmap. Company leaders loved the ease and simplicity of Social Impact Culture Type as a litmus test for prioritizing corporate giving, volunteer opportunities, buying tables at events, launching canned food drives, responding to employee requests for support, and much more.

"Our Social Impact Culture Type gives us a strong yes and a strong no," said one executive. "Armed with the data from the Social Impact Platform, it's much easier to sort through the hundreds of 'doing good' opportunities that come our way every year. Not to mention celebrating the data itself in our marketing materials and on our website."

Time for Your Own Reality Check?

1. Are you finding it difficult to recruit employees who are excited about your growth, goals, culture, and expectations for performance?

2. Is it a challenge to retain and develop your talented employees?

3. Are you looking for ways to inspire your employees to be more productive, happy, and engaged?

If you answered *yes* to any one of these, don't hesitate! Go to socialimpactplatform.com right now to learn more and sign up for the Social Impact Culture Type tool for your organization or company.

10 WAYS TO DO GOOD QUICK REFERENCE GUIDE

CARING
Acting on a commitment to your own physical and mental health.

GIVING
Contributing money or stock to a charitable organization recognized by the IRS.

VOLUNTEERING
A hands-on contribution of your time to an organized cause that helps others.

SERVING
Being active on a board of directors or similar group for a community or civic purpose.

PURCHASING
Buying products and services that include a charitable element.

RECYCLING
Furthering a sustainable and regenerative environment.

DO GOOD, *Feel Better*

DONATING
Collecting necessities for people in need.

MARKETING
Promoting a cause to encourage other people to support it.

SHARING
Helping one particular person, family, or group of people you select.

CELEBRATING
Supporting favorite causes by showing up at events.

SOCIAL IMPACT PERSONALITY TYPE QUICK REFERENCE

Activator

"Activators" are passionate about participating in the causes they care most about, and tend to focus on "changing the world" and impacting one or more social issues on a broad scale.

Connector

"Connectors" prefer to engage in social impact activities that are social in nature, involving the opportunity to get together with other people, although not necessarily in pursuit of a specific charitable endeavor.

Investor

"Investors" prefer to engage in social impact activities that are independent and do not require scheduling dedicated time or working directly with others in the pursuit of a charitable endeavor.

CRASH COURSES: EDUCATIONAL ARTICLES ON SOCIAL IMPACT

As we wrapped up our research, we published a series of educational articles to dive deeper into specific subjects related to social impact and the 10 Ways to Do Good. The articles are reprinted here as brief, easy-to-understand summaries to help you review and actually use the material in *Do Good, Feel Better*.

We've organized the articles into five categories, so you can quickly find tutorials that approach social impact from the perspective that best fits you:

Success

Connect the Dots Between Social Impact and Your Work

Lifestyle

Get Inspired to Celebrate Social Impact as Part of a Well-Rounded, Healthy Life

Community

Discover Ways to Connect with Your Favorite Causes

Money

Learn about the Nuts and Bolts of Social Impact and How It Fits into Your Personal Finances

Family

Handy Tips for Getting Your Kids and Family Involved in Social Impact

Finally, all of these articles are available online for easy sharing with your colleagues and friends. Email us at info@ goodcelebrated.com and request a password to access the articles so you can put the material to good use in your life, work, and community.

Enjoy!

SUCCESS

CONNECT THE DOTS
BETWEEN SOCIAL IMPACT AND YOUR WORK

● ● ●

Do Good in the Community, Do Better at Work

Let's hear it for muddy boots. Making a difference in the workplace is more important than ever to today's emerging talent. In fact, one of the most common statements by today's recruits is that they want to work for an organization whose leaders understand that lives are improved by tapping into the power of doing good for others and making them better at their jobs, all at the same time.

For today's employees, "doing good" is more than just a fun perk. It's a workplace imperative that drives business performance. But are the numbers showing it? According to the latest studies, the answer is a strong yes.

1. **A social impact culture is a must**. Studies of the emerging workforce, including Deloitte's third annual Millennial Survey of nearly 7,800 Millennials from twenty-eight countries, show that a clear majority of the younger talent base wants to work for companies that are committed to charitable giving, volunteering, and making a positive impact on the bottom line and beyond. For example, the 2014 Millennial Impact Study showed that 94 percent of

people in this demographic want to use their talents for doing good.

2. **Doing good drives performance**. Researchers at the University of Southampton found that workers' performance increased by an average of 13 percent when they were given social incentives, and companies with the highest levels of employee engagement report increases in business performance, improving an average of 19.2 percent in operating income.

3. **Social impact is the sticky factor**. A strong culture of engagement can reduce staff turnover by 87 percent. That adds up to some serious cash, considering that it costs an average of two to three times a salary to replace a worker.

Today's workplace experience is about meeting the bottom line—and much more. It's about celebrating the power of doing good to improve personal and organizational performance, leading to better results for everyone—the employees, the business, and the community.

● ● ●

A Closer Look at Social Impact and Today's Executive

In today's socially conscious economy, three realities of "doing good"—social impact—are facing every business leader:

1. Executives know they have to do something about it. Several market pressures demand it: regulatory influences,

sustainability trends, consumer preferences, corporate governance standards, philanthropic solicitations, and expectations of employees and recruits.

2. Executives are aware that the social impact activities going on within their companies are not well-organized, and the activities are not aligned with business goals.

3. Executives want to address social impact, but in the least expensive, least disruptive, and most bottom line-focused way possible.

A social impact strategy is the solution. But what does that entail? Here are a few examples:

1. Develop social impact key messages to build image and credibility, extend the reach of existing marketing activities, and add a new dimension to brand engagement strategy.

2. Conduct social impact training to ensure strong alignment of a social impact program with an employee culture that achieves business goals.

3. Inspire an executive team to implement a social impact decision matrix or other formal but simple system to organize, capture, celebrate, and measure evidence of social impact activities to maximize the return on a community engagement budget.

What's your perspective? It may be time to figure that out.

DO GOOD, *Feel Better*

● ● ●

Volunteering, Happiness, and Success at Work

Happier and healthier at work, thanks to a workplace volunteering program? You bet. Volunteer activities are good for everyone—you, your company, and the community. That's what emerging research is beginning to suggest, including a study by the Corporation for National and Community Service that outlines the heart-healthy benefits of rolling up your sleeves alongside your colleagues to help out in the community.

Research shows that doing good does feel good, scientifically speaking. According to studies at the University of California, people categorized as "grateful" reported feeling 25 percent more happiness and energy—and 20 percent less envy and resentment—than ungrateful people. The data tells us that "prosocial spending"—spending money to benefit others—shows positive signs of increasing happiness. Researchers at the University of British Columbia, Simon Fraser University, and Harvard Business School recently found evidence that "how people spend their money" plays a role in happiness; specifically, those who "spend money on others report more happiness." It's true of adults around the world, and both physical and mental benefits are observed. The "warm glow of giving" can even be seen in toddlers.

And it's not just giving money to charity that makes you feel good. In a study conducted at Carnegie Mellon, 200 hours of volunteering per year correlated to lower blood pressure. Other studies have found a health benefit from as little as 100 hours of volunteering a year.

What kind of giving boosts happiness the most? That, according to researchers, would be the categories of "doing good" that are most closely related to satisfying the basic human needs of "relatedness, competence, and autonomy." The list includes donating to a charity of your choice, helping a neighbor, learning a few new recycling protocols, participating in a community event, purchasing a product that helps support a cause that has touched your family, and serving on a committee to share your talent. It's all good, and good for you, too.

● ● ●

Good Work: Three Steps to Starting Your Own Charity

Has starting your own charity ever crossed your mind? If it has, you are not alone. Thousands of new charities are started each year by people who are passionate about causes to help others.

So how can you get started?

Here are three steps to success.

1. **For profit, or nonprofit?** If you've got a cause you're passionate about, first decide whether you want to start a charity, or a business. The rules and tax advantages are different, and so is the way you fund the enterprise. Charities keep the lights on by getting donations. Businesses keep the

lights on by selling goods or services. Either way, you've got to pay employees and run a budget.

2. **The state and the Feds.** If you decide starting a charity is for you, your next step is to set up your legal entity. It's just like starting a business, and you file your articles of incorporation with the state. The forms are a little different for a nonprofit organization. And, unlike a for-profit business, to start a nonprofit, you need to apply to the Internal Revenue Service for an exemption under Section 501(c)(3). This exemption is what allows your organization to be free from paying income tax, and it also allows people to donate to your organization and be eligible for a tax deduction on their own tax returns.

3. **Sell, sell, sell.** Most people who start a charity are passionate about a cause and probably already have programs in place or in mind to help others. The trick, though, is to get out there and share the news about your cause to raise money. It's just like selling, only you are asking for donations to support your good work instead of selling goods or services like you would in a for-profit business.

Remember, there are nearly 1.5 million charities in America, and every single one of them is asking people for money. Making sure your charity stands out is the ticket to success.

● ● ●

Cause Marketing:

Do You Know How This Popular Consumer Trend Is Impacting Your Bottom Line?

Philanthropy continues its rapid rise as a lifestyle trend that's here to stay. According to the IEG Sponsorship Report, total dollars spent by corporate America on cause sponsorships is projected to reach $2 billion in 2016, more than a 3.5 percent increase over last year.

How does the popularity of cause marketing impact the way Americans approach wealth management? Here are three trends in philanthropy and cause marketing that are changing today's approach to delivering financial services.

1. **Social impact as a lifestyle.** Consumers want to celebrate the good they are already doing, whether that's giving to charities, volunteering, serving on boards, recycling, attending community events, sharing with family and friends, or caring about health and wellness. Today's savvy financial advisor understands that doing good is a big part of living a well-rounded life. It's bigger than a checkbook; it's a mindset, both at home and in the workplace.

2. **The power of consumer choice.** The financial services industry is catching on that consumers embrace the opportunity to support the causes they care about, not the causes they are told to support. For a snapshot of this trend,

take a look at the growth of charitable giving vehicles that offer donors free choice, called donor-advised funds. Donor-advised funds have risen dramatically in popularity over the last several years, with donations into these vehicles growing 24 percent in 2014 alone and total assets in these vehicles reaching $71 billion by the end of 2015. For financial advisors, a turnkey donor-advised fund program offers instant credibility with philanthropic clients to boost loyalty and asset retention between generations.

3. **Success through emotional connections.** Cause marketing works because consumers are loyal to companies and service providers that show a human side. For example, according to the Cone Communications/Ebiquity's 2015 Global CSR Study, more than 90 percent of consumers express a preference for brands that support a cause. Surprisingly, even though 98 percent of affluent Americans give to at least one charity a year, only 14 percent of advisors offer philanthropy tools and advice to their clients, according to the 2014 U.S. Trust Study of High Net Worth Philanthropy conducted in partnership with the Indiana University Lilly Family School of Philanthropy.

The bottom line? If you're a financial advisor and you think cause marketing doesn't apply to you, think again. And if you're a consumer, you can be confident that if you're working with the right financial services provider, you will never need to set aside the causes you love.

● ● ●

Social Impact Culture: The Magic of the Un-Raffle

Are you celebrating philanthropy in the workplace? Of course you are!

It's always a great idea to combine "doing good"—giving money to a charity, for instance—with an opportunity for employees to have fun and maybe get something out of it for themselves, too.

So how about a raffle? Great question.

The challenge with raffles and other "games of chance" is that they are highly-regulated activities. Games of chance are considered gambling by federal and state governments and by regulatory agencies like the IRS. This designation impacts taxability and registration requirements. Raffles done wrong can result in legal and criminal liability—even if the purpose is charitable. So, to avoid the hassle, it's a good idea to stay away from raffles and games of chance altogether.

The good news is that you can accomplish your goal in a very similar way, but without the hassle, by doing the following:

1. Launch a contest to benefit a charity, but don't call it a raffle.

2. Allow anyone to enter the contest, whether or not the person pays or donates money. To enter, contestants can drop their business cards in a bowl or write their names on pieces of paper.

195

3. Add an activity to amp up the charitable side. For example, ask people to submit a few sentences about why the cause is important when they submit an entry (with or without money).

4. Select the name of the winner randomly. If you decide to offer a cash prize to an employee, this prize will be treated as a bonus for payroll purposes and taxed accordingly. A tax-free option is to award a "Giving Card" to the winner, where the winner gets to "give" the money to a charity of choice.

5. Celebrate the collective donation to charity by sending the charity not only the money (minus the prize), but also all of the messages written by employees about the cause (with the names stripped). This is a nice public relations boost for the company if you tell the charity that it can use the messages and your company's name in its marketing materials.

The un-raffle. Something new to love about doing good in the workplace.

● ● ●

Good Company? Listen for These Three Clues

Is your employer in touch with its good side? Research indicates that a phenomenon called "Social Impact Culture Type" is gaining influence on personal achievements and satisfaction at home and in the workplace. How can you tell whether the company you work for is living up to the expectations of today's workforce?

Here are three things you're likely to hear from a good company.

1. **"We care about you."** When your employer understands your preferences for helping others, you will be better equipped to achieve your own personal and professional success. This is better for your bottom line, not just the company's bottom line. Your employer should demonstrate a strong interest in the ways you personally enjoy doing good in the community, beyond workplace giving and volunteering programs.

2. **"What are your favorite social impact activities?"** Your employer should be asking you about your preferences for social impact activities. These are called the 10 Ways to Do Good: Giving to charities, volunteering, serving on nonprofit boards of directors, celebrating at community events, recycling and respecting a sustainable environment, marketing a favorite cause, donating items of food and clothing, purchasing products that support a cause, sharing with family and friends in need, and caring about health and wellness.

3. **"We are in touch with our Social Impact Culture."** Your employer should be paying attention to whether the overall Social Impact Culture Type of its employee base leans toward Investor, Activator, or Connector. These are the three types of "Social Impact Culture." For clues, check the company's website—especially the "people" or "culture"

sections. You'll quickly get a feel for whether Social Impact Culture is on the company's radar—or not.

● ● ●

100 Questions to Ask About Social Impact in the Workplace

Ever wonder why the social impact and community engagement program in your workplace is the way it is? If you're in charge of the program—or if you wish you were—you'll need to get familiar with the questions people like you are asking about employee engagement through corporate philanthropy and social impact activities. Then, you can start to create even more ways for you and your colleagues to get involved.

Here are 100 questions to help you start sketching out your ideas.

1. How can I quickly check out a charity that is requesting a donation?

2. What are the best websites to review a nonprofit's financials, and is it better to support small charities or large charities?

3. What are the keys to motivating employees to participate in our community engagement program?

4. How should we track employee engagement in the program?

5. Should we have an employee committee, and if we

have one already, how should it operate?

6. What do employees need to know about serving on a nonprofit board of directors?

7. Should we find out which boards our employees already serve on?

8. Are there any risks to the company when an employee serves on a nonprofit board of directors?

9. What happens when certain employees just don't like volunteering?

10. Should we require employee participation in Days of Service?

11. Should we give employees paid time off for volunteering?

12. What advice can I give our employees about planning their charitable giving budgets?

13. What kind of cake should we serve at the kick off for our community engagement program?

14. What's an example of a checklist we can offer employees to show them all the options they have to get involved in the community through the company?

15. Can you show me a few sample marketing materials from a company that is doing a good job of celebrating community engagement?

16. Are bake sales to raise money for charity really making a comeback?

17. What's a good ballpark range for donating to a charity for the first time?

18. How do I engage employees across generations… Baby Boomers, Gen X, Millennials, and beyond?

19. What community engagement activities best appeal to new employees, and what activities are better suited for employees with a long tenure with the company?

20. What is the biggest mistake you've seen a company make related to its community engagement program?

21. Can we ever write a check to an individual employee to carry out a charitable activity?

22. Should our company consider donating assets besides cash? How does recycling fit into our community engagement program?

23. Should our company try to purchase products and services from other companies that are "doing good"?

24. How does cause marketing relate to employee community engagement?

25. Should we ask our employees to share their stories of community involvement as a way to boost brand?

26. Should we list the charities we support on our web-

site, or does that create unintended challenges?

27. Are there ways we can involve employees' children in our community engagement program?

28. Can you tell me a funny story about a community engagement program?

29. What is the best way to train our employees quickly about the company's community engagement program?

30. What items should be "off limits" for a canned food drive?

31. Should we offer incentives for an employee's participation in our community engagement program, such as dollars for doers?

32. What are employees' favorite charities and why?

33. What do I need to know about "adopt-a-family" campaigns in the workplace?

34. What's the advantage of donating food, clothing, and necessities over cash, or vice versa?

35. How frequently should we consider doing a "drive" for clothing, canned goods, or necessities?

36. Where can I find a few suggestions for ways to engage our employees across the seasons—spring, summer, fall, winter?

37. What are some websites I can look at to get examples of companies doing innovative things with their community engagement programs?

38. Are there red flags I should look at when I am researching charities for our employees and company to support?

39. Should I worry about funding a single charity for too many years in a row?

40. How well should I know the executive director at our largest grantee charity?

41. How can I use employees' Social Impact Personality Types to increase retention?

42. What data points do employees want to see about their own involvement in the community?

43. How does our community engagement program support our overall wellness program?

44. What are the unique characteristics of community engagement messaging across genders?

45. How can I make sure our community engagement program reflects our company's commitment to diversity?

46. What's the best community engagement message to use when we are recruiting?

47. Should our company start its own charity?

48. Do we need to select a primary corporate cause for our community engagement program to look legitimate?

49. Should the charities we support align with our business in some way?

50. How should I be evaluating a charity's financials?

51. Do I need to worry about a charity that supports a controversial social issue?

52. How can we make sure we are supporting the CEO's favorite charity—without looking like we are playing favorites?

53. Should we support schools and religious organizations?

54. How can I leverage the holiday giving season to improve workplace culture?

55. Is there a best time of year to launch or reboot our community engagement program?

56. Is there a way to incorporate employees' birthdays into our community engagement program?

57. How can our community engagement program balance and respect the affluence of some employees with the challenged economic circumstances of other employees?

58. Should we encourage or discourage employee-driv-

en fundraising activities, such as walks, runs, and bake sales?

59. Should the company endorse and support disaster relief efforts, both locally and nationally?

60. How can I better understand the executive suite's perspective on philanthropy?

61. How can I make it easy for our CEO to show leadership of the community engagement program while still respecting his or her time?

62. What reports should I deliver to our corporate leadership to show results from our community engagement program?

63. What are the opportunities and pitfalls of incorporating social media into our community engagement program?

64. Should our LinkedIn page reflect our community engagement program?

65. Should we have a separate Twitter handle for community engagement?

66. How can I work with our marketing department in leveraging our community engagement program to drive brand?

67. What support should I expect from our marketing department for collateral materials about our program?

68. What is the best way to capture our program on the company website?

69. How should I handle employee requests to support a brand new charity?

70. When is it okay to tell an employee no to a community engagement idea?

71. How much weight should our program place on employee involvement as a measure of success?

72. Should I be using the word "philanthropy," or is that off-putting to employees?

73. Should we name our community engagement program?

74. Why are T-shirts so effective to boost a community engagement program's success?

75. What are the easiest, fastest ways for an employee to get involved in the community?

76. What happens if an employee simply doesn't want to participate?

77. What are the risks of a "corporate cram down" approach to community engagement?

78. What's the best professional focus for our community engagement meeting agendas?

79. What do I need to know about buying tickets and ta-

bles to galas and golf tournaments?

80. What part of a charity event ticket is deductible? How can I achieve more success with filling tables?

81. What are the best ways to engage the "Investor" Social Impact Personality Type of employee?

82. What are the best ways to engage the "Connector" personality?

83. What is my Social Impact Personality Type, and does it correlate to my Myers-Briggs type?

84. What's up with the "Activator" personality and can I ever truly engage people with this personality?

85. Should our company set up a donor-advised fund? Is a corporate foundation the way to go?

86. What's the best way to budget for a community engagement program and donations to charity?

87. Do I need to talk with our executive team about "impact investing," and what is it?

88. Should our community engagement program include scholarships?

89. Is "civic engagement" an out-of-date term?

90. How do I show that our community engagement program improves the bottom line?

91. Should we stop supporting charities that don't write us

thank you notes?

92. What is going through the minds of today's employees as they check out socially-conscious employers?

93. What are the three things I need to know about the tax impact of giving to charity?

94. Where can I find professionals who are qualified to answer these questions?

95. How can I increase participation in our matching gifts program without breaking our budget?

96. What's the best way to track a matching gifts program?

97. What's a good target for our overall community engagement budget based on other companies like us?

98. How can I plan community engagement activities throughout the year?

99. How much of our community engagement program should be tracked online?

100. What are the three most important statistics I absolutely need to know about social impact in the workplace?

● ● ●

Look for These Clues to Solve the Social Impact Mystery

If you're a leader in your company who is responsible for

improving employee productivity, recruiting, and retention, how can you figure out whether your workplace could use a little tune up on its approach to social impact activities and community engagement?

Here are nine clues to help you solve the mystery.

Clue #1: The Self-Appointed Director of Recycling

Who's in charge of going green at your company? Do you know? Is there such a person? Maybe it's nobody. Maybe it's even you! In lots of companies, employees are doing everything they can to create a socially-responsible lifestyle in the workplace to match the socially-responsible lifestyle they lead outside of work. And that includes respecting the environment. It's not uncommon for leadership to emerge from within the employee base, with two or three employees making sustainability their personal mission, sending out email reminders to turn off lights, ensuring that every desk has a recycling bin right next to it, even replacing plastic forks and knives in the break room with real silverware to cut down on waste. In light of the fact that 86 percent of young employees say they would consider leaving an employer if the company's social impact values no longer met their expectations, self-appointed employee leadership can be a very good thing in a company. But how can an employer encourage employee leadership and still keep the business humming along, optimizing human resources toward the company's bottom line? That is the question! How do you know whether your company needs a formula for social impact success? A self-appointed director of recycling just might be your first clue.

Clue #2: Your Inbox Isn't Big Enough Anymore

Are you getting more and more letters and emails asking your company to support worthy causes? Do invitations to charity events land in your inbox almost every day? Do some of these requests come from important clients and customers? Do some even come from employees in your own company? How do you know which causes are worth supporting? You are not alone! The number of nonprofit organizations is increasing steadily, at the rate of nearly 30,000 new organizations each year. The total number of nonprofit organizations in America now totals over 1.5 million! No wonder your inbox is filling up. Your inbox isn't likely to be empty anytime soon. The socially-responsible lifestyle is here to stay—at home and in the workplace. Indeed, 83 percent of consumers are willing to change their consumption habits if it can help make tomorrow's world a better place to live in. But that doesn't mean you can't regain control. Optimizing your social impact budget is a great place to start. By streamlining your company's employee engagement and social impact activities, you'll be better able to meet your budget goals and improve employee and brand engagement at the same time. How do you know whether your company needs a formula for social impact success? Your inbox might be your second clue.

Clue #3: Your Program Isn't Popular

Got a matching gifts program at the company? Lots of good companies do! A matching gifts program can be a terrific part of a corporate community engagement program. Why is it, then, that the average participation in employee matching gifts programs is only 7 percent? Especially considering that 88 percent of new job seekers choose employers based on strong corporate social responsibility values. The truth is that employee matching gifts programs often aren't structured the way employees wish they were. Is the program a genuine employee benefit, designed to celebrate the causes that are most important to the employees? Or is the purpose of the program to direct employees to give to the company's favorite causes? Either purpose can work. The trouble is that most companies don't know which purpose is best for the company. So there's just no clarity, for anyone. But it doesn't have to be that way. A social impact program framework can help determine which elements your social impact program should include and how to divide the roles and responsibilities for the program in your company. The right structure for your social impact program will increase employee participation, improving employee and brand engagement and fostering the socially-responsible lifestyle in your company, a priority for today's employees and customers. How do you know whether your company needs a formula for social impact success? If your program isn't popular, you might be onto your third clue.

Clue #4: To Brag or Not to Brag. Is That Your Question?

Your company is doing a lot! You sponsor charity and civic events. You give employees time off to volunteer. You donate to your customers' favorite causes. Your recycling program was up and running long before recycling was popular. Every member of your executive team serves on at least one community board or committee. Your pro bono work and product donations increase every single year. But should you talk about it? Is it too self-serving to celebrate all of that doing good by mentioning it in your public relations and marketing communications? If that's your question, good for you! Humility is a good thing! But what if you could stay humble and share your stories, too? Impossible? No way! Not if you've aligned your social impact program with the company's mission. When it comes to social impact, figuring out the best mission—for the company, its employees, its customers, and the community—is a best practice, practically guaranteed to give you the ability to do good, stay humble, and spread the word. All at the same time. How do you know whether your company needs a formula for social impact success? If "to brag or not to brag" is your question, you can be pretty sure you've found your fourth clue.

Clue #5: You've Got CMC (Cause Marketing Confusion)

You see it everywhere! Companies and brands aligning with causes. And promoting it, everywhere. In advertising. In office and retail locations. On packaging labels. In new product promotions. All over social media. Even sometimes wrapped up in the brand itself. Feeling a little left out? Not sure where to begin? Not sure cause marketing is a fit for your company? Don't worry. If you've come down with a case of cause marketing confusion, you're in good company. Literally. Plenty of top-notch businesses have yet to add cause marketing to their to-do lists. For very good reasons, too. What if the company selects a cause that backfires, making customers and employees mad instead of happy? What if the cause has a bad reputation you weren't aware of? What if the company spends more money on the cause marketing parts of the product or service than the profit it makes? All very good questions! A case of cause marketing confusion might turn out to be a very good thing. It means you are taking your time, weighing your options, looking at return on investment, and determining whether your business really needs cause marketing as part of its social impact and community engagement program. The answer may be yes. The answer may be no. Either one can work, and work well. But without the analysis, you'll never know whether you picked the right answer. How do you know whether your company needs a formula for social impact success? If you've come down with a case of cause marketing confusion, congratulations. You've stumbled onto your fifth clue.

Clue #6: Where Did This Foundation Come From?

It happens. Someone in the office is cleaning out a filing cabinet, recycling old papers, creating space, decreasing the carbon footprint. All good! And that someone stumbles on an important-looking file. A file that doesn't appear to have been touched for a while. As in a few years. "Do we have a corporate foundation?" that someone asks. "I've never heard of it." Where did that foundation come from? Perhaps it got lost in the shuffle of the merger. Or maybe the person in charge of the foundation retired last year and it's just never been reassigned. Or maybe a handful of people know all about it, but everyone else is in the dark. It happens! And it's okay. Because something can be done. Build an action plan for your corporate community engagement or social impact program, including activities, program structure, timeline, budget considerations, and roles and responsibilities to create an effective socially-responsible lifestyle for your company. Make sure your roadmap reflects best practices in social impact. And that includes mission alignment with the company's business, strategic selection of causes, efficient program structure, employee engagement, measuring progress, and communicating success. Corporate foundations are easy to manage if you have a plan. But they're not so fun if you don't. How do you know whether your company needs a formula for social impact success? Got a foundation that doesn't fit? That's a pretty good clue.

Clue #7: When You Whiteboard Employee Engagement, You Get Modern Art

Oh my. It makes no sense. It's all over the board. It's modern art. Wellness. Volunteer hours. Dollars for doers. Serving on boards. Going green. Selling Girl Scout cookies and golf tournament tickets. Fundraising campaigns. Matching gifts. Employee satisfaction surveys. Strategic planning processes. Team-building retreats. Canned food drives. Jeans day. Taking up a collection for an ill colleague. Put it all up on a whiteboard and it looks like modern art. Or alphabet soup. Or just plain chaos. Chaos isn't always a bad thing. It means you've got lots of enthusiastic employees who are excited about giving to charity. And volunteering. And leading. And recycling. And taking care of themselves and others. But chaos simply is not an effective social impact plan. Chaos won't get your company the employee and brand engagement it's looking for. A social impact program should follow best practices if it's going to be as successful as it deserves to be. That means defining the program. And setting goals. And building a framework. And a roadmap. And implementing it to get measurable results. How do you know whether your company needs a formula for social impact success? If you get modern art when you whiteboard employee engagement, you've discovered a pretty big clue.

Clue #8: Where's the Glue?

Virtual offices. Remote workstations. Flex time. Multiple locations. Your employees are spread all over the place! What's the glue that will hold them together, creating the corporate culture of success you know you need for the company to succeed? That's where social impact activities can come in handy. Get your employees involved—on your terms. What's hot when it comes to engaging employees in a social impact program? Surveying employees is a great place to start. That way, you can determine existing and potential levels of engagement in a corporate giving program and set your goals accordingly. You can even start an employee giving campaign to engage everyone in a handful of strategic causes that bolster the company's market position. Or perhaps consider establishing a birthday program for employees to celebrate each person's gifts to the community. Or start up an employee education program about how your employees can make the most of doing good. And it doesn't have to break your budget. Social impact. Employee engagement. You have to do both. Why not combine the two and get the most bang for your buck? How do you know whether your company needs a formula for social impact success? Maybe the missing glue is a clue.

Clue #9: What Happened to All the Talent?

How's it going, acquiring top talent? And retaining that talent? How successful are you when it comes to getting the kind of people your company needs to stay at the top of its industry? If you're not attracting and retaining the stars, maybe it's because you don't have the right social impact plan. After all, 88 percent of new job seekers choose employers based on strong corporate social responsibility values. And 86 percent of these employees would consider leaving if the company's corporate social responsibility values no longer met their expectations. Employees—and consumers—want a socially-responsible lifestyle, at home and in the workplace. They want to give money to favorite charities. And volunteer time to a favorite cause. And recycle, helping to keep the environment sustainable. And serve in leadership roles, like nonprofit boards and committees at kids' schools. They want to buy products that support a cause. And care for people in need. And care for themselves and their families. Working for good companies—doing business with good companies—is a must-have in any socially-responsible lifestyle. How do you know whether your company needs a formula for social impact success? If you're wondering what happened to all the talent, that might just be your biggest clue.

LIFESTYLE

GET INSPIRED TO CELEBRATE SOCIAL IMPACT AS PART OF A WELL-ROUNDED, HEALTHY LIFE

● ● ●

Questioning Cause Marketing? Here Are the Answers

Are you frequently asked to consider a donation to a cause when you purchase a product? Or are you enticed to purchase a product because the brand supports a particular cause? Either way, you are not alone.

The idea of connecting a cause to a brand for purposes of selling products to consumers is called "cause marketing," and it's been around for more than forty years. And it's here to stay. Cause sponsorship increased nearly 5 percent between 2012 and 2013, and 3.4 percent between 2013 and 2014, according to the IEG Sponsorship Report. Cause marketing is as American as burgers and fries.

The beginning of an expansion beyond cause marketing is happening because the philanthropic marketplace itself has changed, and best practices now freely encourage people to support the causes they care about, beyond the causes they are told to support—by brands or anyone else. Consumers—especially women—want more out of their philanthropic experiences with the brands they love. Consumers want their favorite brands to care about them. And that includes helping consumers celebrate the good they are already doing, whether that's giving to charities, volunteering, serving on boards, recycling, attending community events, sharing with family and friends, or caring about health and wellness.

So what to do when you're hit with cause marketing? We've got three tips.

1. **"No pressure."** Don't feel pressured to give to a cause you don't care about. Best practices in philanthropy have shown for over a decade that giving actually goes up when the charity marketplace helps people give to what they want to give to, without pressure to change favorite causes or add causes that simply are not of interest. The consumer products marketplace is finally catching on to the idea that authentic engagement in social impact is the process that works best to keep consumers happy when it comes to cause.

2. **Care about the brand that cares about you.** Keep an eye out for brands that understand authentic consumer engagement in social impact—brands that help you celebrate the good you are already doing. Savvy companies have figured out how to celebrate the good their employees are already doing, above and beyond the opportunities for community engagement offered by the company itself.

3. **Shop, show, and tell.** When you're with your kids, take advantage of the opportunity to share with them why you care about the causes you care about. In other words,

tell your own story of giving so your children can begin to create their own stories about favorite causes and become savvier consumers in the process. For example, if you pick up a pint of Ben & Jerry's ice cream, and you are passionate about the growing consumer movement for mandatory GMO labeling, tell your kids all about it. "We are buying this ice cream because it is good, and also because the brand believes what we believe about the right to know what's in our food supply."

The bottom line? It's your money. And it's your choice of charities. And that's a cause worth celebrating.

● ● ●

The Rise of Social Impact Messaging in Consumer Engagement

What is "authentic social impact engagement"? And what does it mean for traditional cause marketing? We think that is a very good question, especially as it relates to female consumers.

The drivers of consumer action in the social impact arena are fundamentally different from the drivers of consumer action in a purely commercial setting. A deliberate process of affirmation, education, inspiration, and motivation is the key to generating action-oriented engagement that leads to brand loyalty and repeat buying.

For four decades, cause marketing has been a firmly-rooted method for businesses to improve public relations, increase customer engagement, and create additional marketing opportunities. But is cause marketing alone the most effective method for a business to drive a return on investment from "doing good"? Emerging research suggests that brands can dramatically enhance the results of cause marketing strategies through an "authentic social impact engagement" process.

An intensive consumer research study of mothers and children is beginning to isolate pivotal data points and key consumer perspectives related to the power of social impact messaging. This research will begin to inform marketing teams at consumer products companies who intend to deploy social impact-based strategies to drive a greater emotional connection between the female consumer and the brand.

In the study, mothers of one or more children under the age of eighteen were asked to complete a "10 Ways to Do Good" arts and crafts exercise with their children. The project was designed to celebrate the good that the families were already doing—regardless of the causes supported. Following the exercise, mothers were asked to complete a brief online tutorial about the 10 Ways to Do Good.

Here's the bottom line. (Well, three bottom lines.)

When asked at the conclusion of the research study: "If there were products on the market today that helped you engage with your family in one or more of the 10 Ways to Do Good, how likely would you be to purchase those products?" 85 percent answered, "Yes," they would be likely to purchase those products.

CRASH COURSES: LIFESTYLE

When asked at the conclusion of the research study: "Are you likely to use part or all of the material in the survey to help teach your children or grandchildren, eighteen years of age or younger, about the 10 Ways to Do Good?" 100 percent answered, "Yes."

When asked at the conclusion of the research study: "Do you feel like you have a better mental picture of the day-to-day activities that are part of your overall 'social impact'—how you are making a positive difference in the lives of other people?" 91 percent answered, "Yes."

Wow. With numbers like that, it only made sense that the research team had to go deeper, by conducting sixty-minute individual interviews with participants. And the results were equally powerful:

- "I want a company to acknowledge my current situation as it relates to social impact."

- "I want a company to understand my need to educate my children about doing good."

- "I want a company to inspire me to involve my children in doing good."

- "I want a company to motivate me by making it easy for me to involve my children in doing good."

How's that for the power of consumer engagement through social impact messaging? We're sold.

● ● ●

Rolling Up Your Sleeves—It's on a Roll

Volunteering is becoming a popular leisure activity as social impact becomes an increasingly important part of a well-rounded life.

"Doing good" is on the rise in communities across America. And there are lots of ways you can do it, including giving to a favorite charity, serving on a nonprofit board of directors, recycling and respecting a sustainable environment, and purchasing products that support a cause.

If "doing good" is something you like to do, it probably won't surprise you that volunteering is up, too, with more than 25 percent of adults reporting that they volunteer for at least one nonprofit organization, adding up to more than $173 billion in total value of annual volunteer service hours across the country.

According to recent studies, though, you're probably doing even more to help others than you think you are. Surprised? Here's why:

1. More than 138 million Americans (62.5 percent) engage in either formal or "informal volunteering" in their communities, which includes things like watching your neighbors' kids, helping out friends in need with their grocery shopping, or house sitting for a colleague who is out of town.

2. More than two-thirds (68.5 percent) of Americans share a meal with their family virtually every day.

3. Three out of four Americans (75.7 percent) see or hear from friends and family at least a few times a week.

Do these things count as making a difference? You bet. The emerging definition of "doing good" celebrates the positive benefits of philanthropy for both the giver and the receiver. This means any activity that involves showing you care about other people is not only good for them, but also good for you. It's called "prosocial behavior," and studies have shown it elevates mood and improves overall health.

You're so good! Feels good, doesn't it?

● ● ●

Selfie for a Cause?

You love doing good. Donating to a charity of your choice, helping a neighbor with groceries, learning a few new recycling protocols, attending a community event, purchasing a product that supports a cause that has touched your family, serving on a committee to share your talent. It's all good, and you're doing a lot of it.

But what happens when you combine the power and influence of today's social media with the increasing importance of community impact? That's when things get interesting because you can be a part of winning over the hearts and minds of today's socially-conscious generation. It's called a Social Impact Story (or you can call it a Social Impact Selfie), and nearly everyone has one.

Here's how to share yours, in three easy steps:

1. **Start with an inventory**. You are probably doing more good than you think you are. There are ten ways to do good, not just one or two, and they all count. Giving to a charity of your choice, volunteering for a favorite cause, recycling and respecting a sustainable environment, attending community events, and donating necessities are just a few of the ten ways. Start checking your good boxes and pick a couple where others can help, too.

2. **Find a hook**. Okay, so you're involved. What's a quick data point that will inspire your family, friends, and colleagues to join you for that 5K, food drive, school committee, or fundraiser? The best statistics are those that describe the impact of your activities. So, for example, "I recycled fifteen cans of Diet Coke this weekend," or "My kids and I delivered Rice Krispies treats to thirty people at the nursing home," or "We're giving $5 a month to feed a child overseas." Numbers matter!

3. **Now, share your story**. What's your favorite social media tool? Is it Facebook? Twitter? Instagram? Or email? Text? Even an old-fashioned phone call? Start sharing your message with enthusiasm, and you'll inspire others to make a difference, too.

● ● ●

Your Good Side:
Getting in Touch with Your Social Impact Personality Type

Social connections and community impact are two of today's hottest cultural trends. Combined, they add up to a growing commitment to social impact all across America. But not everyone likes to "do good" in exactly the same way.

What's your ideal social impact activity profile? It depends on your personality.

Research indicates that most people trend toward one of three social impact personality types. All three personality types are based on the types of social impact activities that best fit your lifestyle and your preferences for making a difference in the lives of others.

"Investors" prefer to engage in social impact activities that are independent and do not require scheduling dedicated time or working directly with others in the pursuit of a charitable endeavor.

"Connectors" prefer to engage in social impact activities that are social in nature, involving the opportunity to get together with other people, although not necessarily in pursuit of a specific charitable endeavor.

"Activators" are passionate about participating in the causes they care most about, and tend to focus on "changing the world" and impacting one or more social issues on a broad scale. Activities generally require focused, scheduled, and structured behavior oriented toward a task or community goal.

Which one are you? Getting in touch with the ways you like to give back means you'll enjoy your community engagement even more. And that's good for the community—and good for you, too.

● ● ●

Springtime, Kids, and Going Green

Spring is the perfect season to think about fun things like spring cleaning, gardening, making summer plans and, of course, going green. Recycling and respecting a sustainable environment are terrific ways to do good. Especially after a long, chilly winter. Get your family involved because going green is especially lots of fun for kids.

Here are four easy ways to get started.

1. **Take an inventory of all things green.** Walk around your house with your children and point out where your family is already going green. Have a little fun, marking the spots with big green Xs. You might be surprised to find out just how good and how green you already are! Energy-saving light bulbs for your fixtures. Re-usable bags in your pantry. The thermostat set on a timer to save on electricity. Organic produce in your refrigerator. See? You are so good!

2. **Study your recycling bin and learn where things go.** What are the rules for recycling? Check out the top of your re-

cycling bin in the garage, and then go through your trash to find boxes, cans, and cardboard. Your kids won't mind getting a little dirty. Talk about what makes each item recyclable. This one is useful for adults, too. Bet you learn something you didn't know!

3. **Read books with your kids about the environment and recycling.** The environment and recycling are not always topics your kids would pick on their own, but you will be surprised to see how much they enjoy them. Going green feels good at any age.

4. **Bake something with a hint of green.** Try something new in your kitchen, such as a touch of organic next time you bake a cake or make cookies by adding a garnish of edible, organic flowers as a finishing touch to the layer of frosting.

● ● ●

You've Got Personality!
Why Do "Investor" Types Love Donor-Advised Funds?

Personality type matters, even when it comes to supporting community causes. "Social impact personality type" is especially important to identify whether a donor-advised fund—sometimes called "DAF" for short—is a good fit for a family or an individual to organize gifts to charities.

Why does it matter? It matters because donor-advised funds are the fastest-growing philanthropic planning vehicle in today's wealth-management marketplace. Donor-advised funds are popular because they allow an individual or family to make a tax-deductible transfer that qualifies as a charitable contribution, and then later recommend gifts to favorite charities from the fund when the time is right. A donor-advised fund operates a lot like a checking account just for charity, except it's established according to the IRS guidelines that create the tax advantages.

Not everyone is a fit for a DAF. Research strongly suggests that each of us has a social impact personality type—investor, connector, activator, or a combination—that influences the way we prefer to make a difference in the lives of others through philanthropy and community engagement. Research further suggests that the social impact personality type referred to as "investor" is typically a good match for setting up a donor-advised fund. Activators, who like to focus on a particular cause, are also well-suited for a DAF, but they usually take longer to make the move. Connectors enjoy the social aspects of giving and might not immediately see the benefits of organizing their giving through a DAF.

If you're the investor type, you probably enjoy acting independently as much or more than you enjoy "doing good" with a group. You look at the bottom line when you invest in the community, both from the perspective of your own financial objectives as well as those of the nonprofit organization you support. In other words, you're looking at charitable giving and social impact as an investment to improve the lives of others, and you want to maximize results not only for the people you intend to help, but also for your own tax and estate planning portfolio. Investors love the elegance of the donor-advised fund to achieve many goals through one vehicle.

Investor, activator, connector. Everybody's got a good side. What's yours?

● ● ●

Better Buying:
Shopping, Giving, and Making a Difference

Last year, Americans gave a record $373.25 billion to charities, up 4 percent from the year before. So have you ever wondered how much of that giving happens at the cash register? The answer is almost $400 million, and that number is on the rise.

Here are three things you need to know about making a contribution to charity when you're doing your grocery shopping or visiting your favorite retailer.

First, if you enjoy giving at the register, you are not alone. At some point, 72 percent of American consumers have done it, and 65 percent felt positively about the retailer after they made the gift.

Second, if you don't give at the register, you might be one of the 44 percent of non-givers who take a pass simply because they don't know anything about the cause. That's a perfectly legitimate reason not to give. Focusing on the causes you love is the best way to do good for others and make sure you feel good, too.

Third, don't forget that there's another way to shop and give. Look for brands where a portion of every purchase goes to support a cause. TOMS Shoes has made this famous with its "One for One" program where every item purchased helps a person in need.

As always, remember that giving money to charities is not the only way to "do good." Each person has a unique "Social Impact Personality Type." Some types enjoy doing good in ways that don't necessarily involve spending cash. Other ways to do good include volunteering, recycling, serving on boards, donating food and clothing, celebrating at events, sharing with people in need, marketing a favorite cause, and even caring for your own health and wellness.

● ● ●

Getting Real:
The Power of "Authentic Social Impact Engagement"

When families embark on a journey to make philanthropy a part of their lives across generations, it often starts with simple concepts: Having fun as a family, getting in touch with nature, being authentic and open about values, donating canned goods or clothing to families in need, recycling cardboard and aluminum cans, celebrating every birthday and holiday with a big cake and a gift to charity, buying wrapping paper from the school fundraiser, contributing to a handful of favorite charities—even eating healthy food and appreciating every peaceful moment. In any household, "doing good" is a powerful way to create a sense of belonging—in the family, the community, and the world.

But is there more to the story? Yes.

A series of pilot studies yielded a process called "authentic social impact engagement." In the social impact arena, the drivers of consumer action are fundamentally different from the drivers of consumer action in a purely commercial setting. Indeed, authenticity is the key to action-oriented engagement by a consumer of philanthropy, whether that consumer is a donor to a nonprofit, a volunteer for a charity, a consumer purchasing a brand that supports a cause, or even a homeowner committed to recycling paper products and aluminum cans.

So what is "authentic social impact engagement"? The formula is based on four parts: Affirmation, Education, Inspiration, and Motivation.

1. **Affirmation:** Before a person can become deeply engaged, emotionally and intellectually, in a community or a cause, or even philanthropy in general, he or she must feel affirmed that what he or she is doing already to "do good" is in fact good. This includes not only giving to charities, of course, but also volunteering in the community, recycling and respecting the environment, donating canned goods, serving on boards of directors or committees, and attending community events. This also includes emerging methods of social impact engagement, such as purchasing products that support a cause, mar-

keting favorite charities through social media, and even committing to personal and family health and wellness. The emerging methods of social impact are particularly important to members of the next generation, who view their social impact as wide-ranging and not restricted to the definition of "charity" according to the Internal Revenue Code. "Affirmation" requires acknowledgment—without judgment—that giving manifests itself in a variety of forms.

2. **Education:** Opportunities for learning about philanthropy are in demand across all audiences. Students are interested in techniques that result in lives actually being changed for the better. Parents want to know how to teach their young children about doing good. Grandparents want to know how to leverage philanthropy to create a multi-generational platform for preserving family values. Young professionals are seeking new ways to access business information about nonprofits, especially online. Corporate executives seek techniques for charitable planning that meet their tax and estate planning objectives. The educational component of community engagement is a rich environment for testing and deploying best practices in philanthropy education to help people understand how philanthropy makes a difference in the quality of life of the people they wish to serve. Note, however, that authentic engagement requires authentic education; education is a process of self-discovery—not a prescription by philanthropy professionals for how to do good the "right" way for the "right" causes.

3. **Inspiration:** Stories are powerful. Stories of people and companies making an impact will inspire others to pursue their own charitable objectives. Certainly the cause selected is an important part of any story. Too often, however, the "giving" side of the equation is left out of the story—the point of view of the person doing the good. How did the experience with philanthropy make the giver feel? How did her life improve? How did the giver's relationships with his children and family get better by pursuing philanthropy together? How did the giver make positive changes to her mental and physical health by integrating philanthropy into her life? How was the giver's life enriched by feelings of gratitude and the ability to help people in need? Generosity empowers the giver, and a story is much more powerful to inspire others when it reinforces that theme.

4. **Motivation:** Motivation is the moment of truth. Does a student, an employee, an executive, or a parent have the tools and information to act on a philanthropic desire? The first key to motivating a person to "do good" and become more involved in philanthropy is to offer easy ideas in step-by-step format so that it does not seem overwhelming. This is especially true for a young professional or a donor in the early stages of philanthropic involvement. These "emerging" philanthropists are typically busy in their careers and family lives. Plus, they are accustomed to multitasking in bite-sized activities, usually conducted online. People at all levels of giving frequently talk about this frustration: "I want to help, but

I just don't know how I can help." It is not useful for a person to be told to "get involved" with nothing specific to back it up—no call to action.

The second key to successful motivation in the social impact space is that people must believe that their acts of doing good, no matter how small, make a difference. "My gift doesn't matter" is often top of mind for people giving money or donating time. Changing that thinking will better motivate people to get involved—on their own terms—in something specific.

Now, are you ready to rethink "doing good"? By isolating a person's relationship with the act of giving itself through the four-step formula for authentic engagement, executives, civic leaders, parents, employees, students—and anyone else engaged in philanthropy—will be more satisfied with the experience. And that's success by doing good.

COMMUNITY

DISCOVER WAYS TO CONNECT
WITH YOUR FAVORITE CAUSE

● ● ●

Can You Count on the Charity You've Never Heard of?

Is it a charity, or is it a mystery? You're wondering whether you can count on the charity to do what it says it will do with the dollars you give. Consider these tips before you write a check to a charity you've never heard of.

Thousands of new charities pop up every single year. So if you feel like you're receiving more and more requests to give to organizations whose names don't ring a bell, you are not alone. Here are three things you can do to make sure your experience with giving is positive when you are trying something new.

1. **Consider the source.** If it's a friend, colleague, or a neighbor asking you to support a cause she knows and loves, you can be more confident in your contribution. Ask about the organization to find out whether it's a fit for you. Don't worry—you won't offend your friend by asking questions. Instead, your interest in the cause your friend is marketing will give her a chance to tell the story about how that organization is making a social impact. Spreading the word is a good thing!

2. **Start with something other than money.** Giving money to a charity is not the only way to do good. Supporting causes includes a wide range of other activities, such as recycling, volunteering, serving on boards, donating canned goods or clothing, attending community events, marketing a favorite nonprofit, sharing with friends and families in need, purchasing brands that support causes, and caring for your own health and wellness. So, if you are uncomfortable with a monetary contribution, do something else for the charity you're being asked to support. Volunteer for an hour or two, donate household items, or attend one of the charity's events by buying a ticket instead of making an outright donation. These activities give you a chance to check things out.

3. **Go online.** Of course, you should check out the charity online. Giving is big business, and charities today know they need to report compelling information on their websites about the difference they're making with your dollars. In 2013, for example, Americans gave more than $335 billion to charities, across a wide range of causes: 47 percent to support religious and educational institutions; 12 percent flowing to human services charities; 11 percent to foundations and donor-advised funds; 10 percent to charities focused on health; and the rest of the dollars flowing to charities focused on the arts, the environment, international causes, and public benefit organizations.

And remember, no matter how you choose to make a social impact, every act of doing good counts, especially when you support the causes you love the most.

● ● ●

Three Steps to Savvy Online Giving

Giving is up, according to the Giving USA report. In 2014, Americans gave a record $355 million to charity. Every year, a bigger percentage of contributions are made through a website. What are the steps you need to take to stay savvy when you give online?

More and more people are choosing to make donations to their favorite charities online, especially on their mobile phones and tablets. Thanks to this increasing "mobile mind-set" when it comes to supporting the causes we love, online giving grew 8.9 percent in 2014 compared to 2013.

So what do you need to know about online giving? Keep these three tips in mind to make sure your experience with online giving is as positive as the difference you intend to make in the lives of others.

1. **Watch for security basics.** Every reputable online giving website, or a specific nonprofit website collecting on-line donations, should make a representation about its security and privacy. Look for the privacy policy on the website, for example, to be sure the organization does not give away your information. Not every website is built by developers with cutting-edge cloud expertise, so keep your eyes open.

2. **Keep that email.** When you make an online donation to a charity registered under Internal Revenue Code section 501(c)(3), you are eligible for an income tax deduction. The email you get back from the charity acknowledging your donation should contain language for you to use when filing your tax return. Don't hit delete without looking closely.

3. **Is it charity, or just doing something good for someone else?** Finally, remember that there are plenty of other types of online giving besides charitable donations. For example, you might be asked to participate in funding a project to help a neighbor with medical bills, collecting donations for a scholarship, or even funding someone's start up idea for a new company. Keep in mind that not all endeavors are organized for charitable purposes, so you might not be able to deduct your investment.

The rules are as easy as 1, 2, 3. So go ahead—enjoy the experience of charitable giving online. You are so good!

● ● ●

Volunteering:
Like It, Love It, Do More of It?

Volunteering is a hands-on contribution of your time to a non-profit organization. Volunteer activities can include just about anything that takes the load off of the staff members at your favorite charity, whether that's serving meals, packing backpacks, or picking up trash on the side of the road. More than 25 percent of adults volunteer each year for a nonprofit organization.

But what if you are in the majority? What if you are among the 75 percent of people who do not regularly volunteer? Here are three tips to make you feel good, whether you choose volunteering as a way to do good, or something else.

First, remember that volunteering, even though it's all the buzz, isn't the only way to do good. Giving to charity, recycling, donating canned goods, purchasing products that support a cause, attending community events, and sharing with colleagues are just a few of the other ways you can give back to the community and celebrate the causes you love the most.

Second, if you'd love to be in that 25 percent of Americans who volunteer but you don't quite know how to get started, social media can come in very handy. Let your friends know that you're up for a day of volunteering, and see what you get back. You're likely to get a handful of good suggestions from experienced volunteers about local organizations. And chances are good those suggestions will come with friends who want to join you.

Third, no matter what, make sure you love what you are doing. Yes, you are making a difference in the lives of others when you get engaged in the community, but you're also making a difference in your own life. And that matters! If you don't like dogs and cats, by all means don't volunteer at an animal shelter. On the other hand, if you really enjoy the satisfaction of stuffing hundreds of envelopes or sorting canned goods, pick that!

It's a simple concept: Do what you love. It's surprisingly simple to forget that doing what you love applies to the ways you do good, too.

● ● ●

Service with a Smile:
Making the Most of Your Nonprofit Board Experience

Serving on the board of directors of your favorite nonprofit organization is a great way to celebrate the cause you love the most and share the gift of your leadership. But is a stint on a board of directors the right move for you? It depends.

Here are three factors you can evaluate to make the decision easier when you are weighing "to serve or not to serve."

1. **Be honest with yourself about what you think the nonprofit organization wants from you.** Is your perspective valuable because you've been personally served by the organization? Is your name well-recognized in the community, making you a magnet for the charity's positive public relations? Does the charity want your money—or want you to ask your friends for money? If in doubt, ask. Having an open conversation with the charity's executive director will help you get clarity about what's expected of you.

2. **Consider what you want for yourself.** Are you interested in getting to know the other people on the board? Do you

want to help improve the charity's financial situation and governance? Are you devoted to the charity and want to give back? There are no wrong answers, but knowing what you want is a key part of ensuring a mutually-beneficial experience.

3. **Remember that the most important part of serving on a board is showing up.** The charity is counting on your smart, objective voice in the board meetings, asking constructive questions, and ensuring that the public's trust in the charity is maintained. Before saying yes, be sure to find out when the meetings are scheduled. Most boards of directors meet at a pre-set date and time several times throughout the year. If you can't make the meetings, you and the charity are both better served by your declining the invitation to serve.

Most of all, do what you love. Whether it's serving on a board, recycling, attending events, giving money, or something else, make sure you like doing it. Doing good, your way, is the best move for you and for your community.

● ● ●

Where Does the Money Go?

When you write a check to a charity or donate online with a credit card, how do you know the organization is putting the money to good use? Here are three tips to make the giving to your favorite charities even better.

1. **Give to what you know.** Most Americans get the greatest joy from giving to causes with which they are personally familiar. This makes it easier to understand how the charity is using your dollars. So, for example, if you've had experience with helping foster children, you are likely to understand how the organization is using your donation to support training for foster parents. Or if someone in your family suffers from an eating disorder, you will understand what it means to give money to support an individual to receive an extra six weeks of treatment beyond what insurance will pay. And do not be afraid to ask! Most organizations are happy to share the tangible impact of your donation—whether it is $10, $100, $1,000 or more.

2. **Give where you are.** Many Americans support charitable causes overseas, and that is wonderful. But don't forget that sometimes the greatest needs are right here at home. Look for opportunities to support local charities who are celebrating year-end giving by offering information about the overall need, the mission they serve to meet that need, and the positive impact of a year-end gift on the lives of others. When you give local, you are in a much better position to have confidence in your gift.

3. **Give to what you love.** Above all, give to the charities you love. Gifts that are aligned with a passion and your own love of humanity carry the most energy and ultimately make the most difference. The bottom line is that giving should feel good. Certainly understanding how a charity is using the money is a part of that. But don't let that get

in the way of doing good and enjoying every minute of it.

● ● ●

Climbing Up:
Routine Is Out, Strategy Is in for Nonprofits and Technology

Philanthropic institutions exist to improve the communities they serve. In philanthropic institutions such as community foundations and other donor-focused nonprofits, serving donors is critical to serving the community. In fact, it comes first.

That's why donor-focused philanthropic institutions zero in on three big goals in their strategic plans:

1. Recruit new donors to start giving or start getting involved in other ways.

2. Engage existing donors even further by encouraging them to give more, inspire the next generation, or get involved in a community initiative.

3. Exercise responsible stewardship of assets, including running a lean operation, meeting budget goals, and maintaining the highest standards of financial and data integrity.

So how does the online experience play into these three goals? That depends. Are you following a routine, or are you being strategic?

Forward-thinking philanthropic institutions view the online experience as an integral part of overall donor engagement. This means they take technology and website decisions very seriously. These nonprofits look for vendors who are strategic partners, not just product and service providers. In other words, the decisions about online experience are anything but routine.

If you're a board member or on the staff of a nonprofit with growth aspirations, don't be tempted to address the evaluation of donor portal and web capabilities as routine technology decisions or boxes to be checked in the hectic pace of managing priorities to a budget. By elevating technology decisions to the level of a top strategic priority, you can help ensure that not only donor satisfaction, but also donor acquisition, donor retention, and staff efficiency are optimized through your technology. Ultimately, technology is what drives your organization's growth and return on investment.

Rise above routine. Technology is strategy.

MONEY

LEARN ABOUT THE NUTS AND BOLTS OF SOCIAL IMPACT AND HOW THEY FIT INTO YOUR PERSONAL FINANCES

● ● ●

501(c) What?

When you think about "doing good," giving to a charity is often the first thing that comes to mind. Giving is as American as swimming in the summertime, with total giving in the United States topping more than $355 billion dollars annually. That's more than 2 percent of GDP.

But what's a "501(c)(3)" anyway? You hear the term all the time, but you might not know what it is.

Here are three tips to clear up the confusion.

1. The first thing to remember is that giving to a charity is not the only way to do good. Doing good includes a wide range of activities, from recycling, to volunteering, to serving on boards, to donating canned goods or clothing, and much more.

2. "Giving," as philanthropy defines it, is an act of doing good that involves contributing money to a charitable organization. The organization, in turn, uses the money to carry out its mission. But giving money to just any orga-

nization doesn't mean you're eligible for a tax deduction. To qualify for a deduction, your contribution must be to an organization that is approved under Section 501(c)(3) of the Internal Revenue Code. This means that the organization meets certain government regulations for having an altruistic purpose that doesn't drive profit for any particular individual or group of individuals.

3. Some acts of giving are better described as "sharing." For example, if you contribute money to help a specific family defray medical costs, or you contribute to a scholarship fund for the children of a friend who has passed away, those contributions are not eligible for a charitable tax deduction because they do not meet the IRS's 501(c)(3) test. That doesn't mean, though, that they aren't wonderful ways to do good and share a little of what you have with another human being who needs help.

After all, the IRS doesn't define "doing good." The IRS can determine what's deductible and what's not, but the ways you do good are up to you.

● ● ●

Is the Cost of that Event Ticket Deductible?

Attending an event to support a favorite cause is a popular way to "do good." And more than 90 percent of Americans give to at least one charity each year or participate in another social impact activity. But when you buy that ticket to a charity event, how do you know how much of it is tax deductible? Here are three tax tips worth learning to be sure you're getting the most bang for your "doing good" buck.

1. Remember that a tax deduction for charitable contributions is possible only if you itemize deductions on your income tax return instead of using the IRS's standard deduction. So before you start worrying about keeping your receipts, check to be sure it matters in the first place.

2. Even if you do itemize your deductions, remember that the IRS only allows a tax deduction for the portion of the ticket price for which you, the giver, received nothing of tangible value in return for your contribution. So, when the charity sends you a receipt for your gift, you'll see that it has subtracted the fair market value of the food, beverage, entertainment, T-shirts, and gifts from the dollar amount of your contribution.

3. Remember that it's not all about the tax deduction. Buying tickets to an event to support your favorite cause is a good thing to do, with or without the deduction. It's always a good thing to do when you're having a good time for a good cause.

● ● ●

Easy Ways to Check Out a Charity

More than 90 percent of American households give to charity each year, volunteer for a favorite cause, or participate in social impact activities in some way. Chances are, you are doing it yourself, maybe even two or three times a year. But how do you know the charity you choose is a good one? That's a good question. And the answer is that you can check out a charity the hard way, or the easy way.

What's the hard way? Lots of research. Visit national online resources, such as Charity Navigator and GuideStar, to see how the charity you are choosing stacks up on its financials, its governance, and the impact of its programs. It's fairly common for donors to want to know the percentage of an organization's budget going to fundraising, for example. Donors also want to know who's on the board of directors—who are the people making sure the charity fulfills its mission in a financially-sound manner?

There's certainly nothing wrong with this level of research.

But there is an easier way. Next time you check out a charity, try these three easy steps and you'll validate your decision every bit as much as if you were to research the cause extensively.

1. **Check out the charity's website.** Does it make sense? Does it look well-organized? Can you find the information you're looking for in five minutes or less? Go with your instincts here. You'll be able to get an excellent feel for the way an organization is run, just by looking at how it presents itself online.

2. **See how quickly you can identify the actual people the charity helps.** Not names, of course, but the group of

people who are benefiting directly from the charity's activities. So, for example, at a children's hospital, you will want to know that children are being well cared for. If it's a homeless shelter you're supporting, scan the website quickly to look for stories and information about specific activities the charity is doing to help those in need, beyond broad generalizations.

3. **Most importantly, ask yourself whether you truly love this cause.** If it feels good to support a cause, that counts for a lot. Giving works best when it's self-defined, and that means defined by you. The results of your giving will be that much better if you support the causes you love, in the ways you choose to support them. Sure, every once in a while, it's okay to support a friend's cause because you care about that friend, but try to stick with your own personal favorite causes as much as you can. Doing good should feel great—to you.

● ● ●

Your Charitable Giving Budget: How Much, How Often, and Who Gets It?

A new year means resolutions, fresh starts, and, of course, budgets.

So how do you factor in your charitable giving? To get started, consider planning your charitable giving budget around three points—amount, timing, and category.

1. **How much?** That's the $64 question. Or more, depending on your budget. The first thing to keep in mind when setting a budget for supporting your favorite causes is that giving money isn't the only way to do good. If your wallet is tight, consider other social impact activities such as volunteering, serving on a board, donating gently-used clothing, purchasing products that support a cause, or marketing your favorite charities through social media. It all counts. Set your annual charitable giving budget based on what makes sense for you and your family.

2. **How often?** Charities are looking for support year round. More than 50 percent of charitable contributions are made during the holiday season, but you don't have to do it that way. Consider spreading your giving throughout the year. Your tax deduction is unaffected, and you'll be giving the organizations you support a much-appreciated boost to cash flow.

3. **Who gets it?** Most people support a wide variety of charities. To see where your dollars are going, try sorting the organizations you support into the major categories of social impact:

   • Community Development
   • Arts & Culture
   • Children & Families
   • Health & Life Sciences
   • Education

Keep in mind that religious giving frequently falls into one of these five categories, depending on your gift's purpose.

Budgeting for social impact can be as easy as 1, 2, 3. And you'll love watching the numbers come alive as you celebrate the causes that you and your family love the most.

● ● ●

Reflections on Recordkeeping:
Is a Donor-Advised Fund Right for You?

Gearing up for tax time and looking everywhere for receipts from your charitable donations? This might be the year to look in the mirror and get real about streamlining your charitable giving recordkeeping. And you can do that through a donor-advised fund.

What's a donor-advised fund? A donor-advised fund is a philanthropic planning tool offered by financial institutions, community foundations, and other nonprofits, including an increasing number of universities and endowments.

And they are popular! Gifts to charities from donor-advised funds grew 27 percent in 2014 to reach $12.5 billion. At the same time, total assets in these accounts have hit an all-time high, topping more than $70.7 billion.

Why are donor-advised funds so popular? A donor-advised fund is a tax-effective, flexible tool to organize giving to charities. The administrative convenience of a donor-advised fund means the tool is becoming a popular alternative to private foundations.

Here's how it works. You set up a donor-advised fund with a community foundation or a financial institution. Then, you transfer cash or appreciated stock into it. Because the donor-advised fund qualifies under Internal Revenue Code Section 501(c)(3), the tax deductible transfer is completed at that point. So you've got the receipt for your tax return next year. Then, over the course of the year—and beyond—you can do your charitable giving directly from the money in your donor-advised fund, making gifts to charities of your choice. The donor-advised fund administrator tracks where you give and how much.

And, best of all, donor-advised funds are built to accommodate all levels of givers, whether you give hundreds of dollars to charity each year, or thousands. After all, every gift to a cause you love makes a big difference in the lives of others, and in your own life, too.

● ● ●

Money with an Impact:
Doing Good and Growing the Bottom Line

As social consciousness in America continues to rise, the gap between "doing good" and "doing well" is narrowing. This trend is affecting every sector of our economy, including the financial sector, which has traditionally focused only on the bottom line. That's changing.

If you're evaluating the best way to approach your commitment to the community as you work with your financial advisor, here are three pointers to bring you up to speed.

1. **"Good" is more than "not bad."** "Impact" and "investing"—used in the same sentence—are becoming popular buzzwords among wealth managers and financial advisors. But what does the term actually mean, and what should the average person know about personal investments and "doing well by doing good"?

   For more than a decade, the financial services industry has marketed what are known as "socially responsible investing strategies." Until now, though, the approach has been mostly focused on excluding stocks and other investments that are seen as "bad," like cigarette companies or manufacturers of alcoholic beverages. Now, savvy financial advisors and wealth managers are building portfolios that recognize and celebrate worthy investment candidates based on the good the companies do—not just for their shareholders, but also for their employees, communities, stakeholders, and the world.

2. **Tools for philanthropy are in high demand.** Leading edge financial advisors and wealth managers offer their clients a broad array of tools to support their clients' charitable giving needs. Tools include not only impact investing options, but also charitable legacy planning, income tax strategies to maximize charitable gifts, and donor-advised funds, which are quickly becoming the charitable planning vehicle of choice.

3. **A little more human, a lot more success.** Finally, today's wealth managers and financial advisors are adopting a more human approach to client service. This means advisors are more in tune with their clients' focus on philanthropy as an integral part of a well-rounded life. This is especially important for engaging the next generation of financial services clients, who are seeking more rewarding experiences at work and in their personal lives as they pursue both financial and community success.

● ● ●

Better Giving:
When Cash Is Out

We've all heard the saying "Cash is king." Most of the time that's a fantastic rule of thumb. But sometimes cash isn't the best way to support your favorite charity. How can you tell? Here are three clues to keep you on the lookout for opportunities to get more bang for your giving back bucks.

1. **Assets vs. Cash.** If you're holding highly appreciated assets, such as stock or real estate, and you are also planning to make a significant gift to charity, consider giving the appreciated assets instead of cash. Why is that? Because assets like appreciated stock can be sold by the charity for 100 cents on the dollar—no capital gains tax applies. That means the charity ends up with more money to work with than you would if you sold that same asset yourself.

2. **Consider a donor-advised fund.** If you want to support several charities all at once, but you have a single large asset you plan to give to the charities, consider using a donor-advised fund to facilitate the contributions. You can transfer the asset to the fund, get the tax benefits, have the asset converted to cash, and then allocate the proceeds to several different charities of your choice.

3. **Think outside the box.** Giving something other than cash means contributing any asset you have that has high appreciation. Even artwork, jewelry, antiques, limited edition books, and other collections can be contributed to your favorite nonprofit.

And, before you get worried it's too complicated, remember, giving anything to charity is worthwhile. Whether you are contributing stock, real estate, books, or even canned food from your pantry, it's all good! Every gift makes a difference to the more than one million charities in the United States that are raising money to support their missions.

● ● ●

"I'll Do It Myself": Next Generation Philanthropy

Tomorrow's philanthropists are fast becoming today's philanthropists. That means the millennial mindset is a rising force in emerging charitable-giving behavior. Has starting your own charity ever crossed your mind? If you've got the millennial mindset, the answer is probably "Yes."

Thousands of new charities are started each year by people passionate about a cause. Millennial or not, if you've got a cause you're passionate about, how do you know whether starting your own charity is right for you?

Here are two key questions to ask yourself before you get started.

1. **Do you really want to start a charity, or is a for-profit structure better for you?** The answer starts with what you want to accomplish. And then you can see what revenue model is best. Either way, you have to ask for money—either by selling a product or service, or asking for people to support your cause. Check out the pros and cons of a nonprofit versus for-profit.

2. **Is there an existing charity already doing something similar?** There are nearly 1.5 million charities in the United States, so chances are pretty good that there is one that does what you want to do. Don't forget that competition for dollars is high. Requests for charitable contributions are filling up everyone's inbox, not just yours! A great idea is to consider incubating your idea as a volunteer within an existing charity to test the idea and get early traction.

Remember, starting a charity is just like starting a business; it's just governed under a section of the tax code with rules relating to the deductibility of donations and the exemption from taxation. You still have to make sure ends meet and that your expenses don't exceed your revenue.

FAMILY

HANDY TIPS FOR GETTING YOUR KIDS AND FAMILY INVOLVED IN SOCIAL IMPACT

● ● ●

Teaching Kids About Helping the Homeless

With homelessness on the rise, panhandling is on the rise, too. That means you are more likely to pull up next to a panhandler at intersections in your community. This creates an especially tricky situation when you are in your car with the kids.

So what should you do? Should you roll down your window and give the person money? Should you ignore the person? Should you report the person to a homeless shelter? These are sticky issues, especially as winter approaches and times get tougher.

Here are three easy tips for putting your mind at ease on this "doing good dilemma."

1. **Do not feel guilty if you don't want to give.** Doing good is highly personal. Studies indicate that philanthropy as an industry will grow beyond its current $355 billion annually only if people give to the causes they care about—in the ways they care about. Whether you choose to "do good" by sharing a granola bar or a $5 bill with a homeless person, give money to your favorite charity, volunteer for a favorite cause, or recycle, it is all good.

2. **Anything you can do to empower another person to help him- or herself is a gift.** People who are in trouble or in despair need to know that they are still valued as human beings. Philanthropy, after all, is a love of humanity that should benefit the giver and the receiver. So, if you are not comfortable rolling down your window, you might consider offering a smile of compassion and respect that says, "You matter." Inspiration and hope are often the best gifts of all.

3. **If your kids are with you in the car, use the opportunity to offer a little education.** Of course, you can share with them how important it is to be safe and careful in the presence of strangers. You can also share information about the needs of others in your own community. For example, according to the Mid-America Regional Council, current estimates put the number of homeless in the five-county Kansas City area at about 13,000 individuals with almost half of them in families. It is important to note that it is not just single men and women who are homeless. Area school districts identify nearly 5,000 homeless school-age children. That's a big number—and your kids will relate to it.

● ● ●

Feeling Good About Doing Good

"How did that make you feel?" We ask our kids that question a lot, usually after something happens that is not so good. A sibling swipes a favorite toy. A friend at school sits at another table at lunch. Your child misses a few too many on a spelling test or gets in trouble for playing rough at the swimming pool.

We have the best intentions, of course. We want our kids to acknowledge that things like this don't feel so good so that they are less likely to copy the behavior.

Positive reinforcement works, too. That's critically important, according to child psychologists. Encouraging a child to acknowledge the good feelings that come from getting an A on a spelling test, showing kindness to others, and sharing with brothers and sisters are powerful tools for motivating repeated good behavior.

So how does all of this work when charitable giving and doing good are involved? It turns out, according to studies conducted at the Greater Good Science Center at the University of California at Berkeley, that the feelings associated with giving money to a favorite charity, volunteering, recycling, donating, sharing, caring, and all of the other ways to do good are also powerful tools for building self-esteem and confidence.

This research is aligned with the most basic notion of "philanthropy," which, according to the classic dictionary definition, means "love of humanity" in the sense of caring, nourishing, developing, and enhancing "what it is to be human" on the part of both the giver and the receiver.

So how does the research play out with real kids? We decided to find out in our own summer experiment. We gave ten little girls a certificate for $10 so that each one could make a donation to a charity of her choice. We asked each girl to give us one word to describe how giving the dona-tion to charity made her feel. What we heard made us smile: "proud," "good," "special," "happy," "glad," "grateful," and "inspired."

Feeling good about giving? Absolutely.

● ● ●

Moms, Kids, and Learning Online

Does your family enjoy giving to the charities you care about? You are not alone! More than 90 percent of Americans give to at least one charitable organization each year or participate in social impact activities in some other way.

But how do families learn about "doing good" in the first place? That's an area that is the subject of increasing atten-tion in academic and empirical studies.

The goal of the emerging research is to identify the motiva-tions and expectations of people who give to charity, espe-cially as the household definition of "philanthropy" expands to include a wide range of giving activities, including dona-tions of gently-used clothing and books, attending communi-ty events, recycling, volunteering, serving on boards, sharing with neighbors, purchasing products that support a cause, caring about your own well-being, and even marketing a fa-vorite organization through social media.

How do families learn to do good? Not surprisingly, the research is beginning to suggest that learning starts with mothers, who work with their children at home. And learning about philanthropy in families also appears to start online.

A study conducted through the Social Impact Benchmark with a pilot group of mothers has revealed that learning about philanthropy may actually be supercharged when mothers combine hands-on activities with online activities. In the study, mothers were asked to complete a "10 Ways to Do Good" coloring activity with their children, designed to celebrate the good that the families were already doing— regardless of the causes supported. Following the exercise, mothers were asked to complete a brief online tutorial about the 10 Ways to Do Good. The study indicated that mothers and future philanthropists were able to increase the richness of their conversations by interacting with traditional "paper and crayon," online resources, and, of course, each other. In fact, more than 92 percent of the study participants indicated that they would even be very likely to reuse the material in the online tutorial to help teach their children about doing good.

So, what's the bottom line? The bottom line is that mothers interacting with children—and leveraging technology to enhance the experience—is a powerful way to teach the benefits of philanthropy in all of its many forms.

Three cheers for Mom! Mothers are so good.

● ● ●

Tips for Seasonal Adopt-a-Family Activities

Adopting a family is a terrific charitable giving activity for donating gifts and necessities to local nonprofit organizations, which then place those items directly into the hands of families who are facing challenges, especially during the holidays or during back-to-school season. There are many options for this traditional form of adopting a family. Search online for "adopt a family" and you'll find dozens of local organizations you can contact to get this done.

But a twist on the traditional idea is gaining popularity. Instead of going out shopping for a family, some people are doing something else to adopt a family—writing a check.

Yes, it's fun to go out shopping for children who need presents or backpacks. But sometimes the nonprofit organizations serving these families need a lot more than gifts for the kids, including social services, medical care, emergency assistance, and money to pay staff and keep the facilities going. All of these things take money, and your donation will be particularly welcome during those times during the year when families have extra expenses.

But does that take all of the fun out of doing good? Just giving money to a charity of choice?

Not if you put together your own "adopt-a-family" package and zero in on exactly the difference you want to make in the lives of others.

CRASH COURSES: FAMILY

This is a wonderful way to teach children about charitable giving, gratitude, and empathy for others. For example, ask your children to imagine the life of another child exactly their age who does not have as much as they have. What would that child need? Money to pay for school lunches? Enough money to go to the dentist? A new sweatshirt? Money for swimming lessons or a pair of glasses? Think about the same question for yourself. If you were not so fortunate, what might you need? Help paying the rent? Counseling services? Someone to help you navigate legal services or Social Security benefits?

Next, do a little research online and find one or two local organizations that meet these needs—especially those same organizations that operate traditional adopt-a-family programs. When you write a check for whatever amount you feel is appropriate and in your budget, send the money with a note about why you decided to make this gift: because you wanted to adopt a family of people just like you—only less fortunate. It's a great story for the nonprofit organization's staff members to share with each other for inspiration and encouragement for the important work they do. Plus, if you want, you can also indicate how you'd like your donation to be spent.

You'll be surprised by how rewarding this activity really is. You're helping people who need it, during seasons when so many of us give and receive so much. And you'll be helping yourself, too, because you will feel so grateful for everything you have.

And remember, no donation is too large or too small. If you can give a little, you have a lot.

● ● ●

Simplify Your Holiday Decisions for Giving to Charities

If you're looking for a way for your family to streamline your decision-making as you sort through the growing stack of charitable-giving opportunities, consider using your Social Impact Personality Type as a filter.

By the way, what's the Social Impact Personality Type of each person in your household? The holidays are a perfect time to find out.

There are three Social Impact Personality Types: Investor, Activator, and Connector. Here's how getting in touch with your good side can help you make funding decisions that are right for you, depending upon which type you are.

If you're an Investor, meaning you like to do good on your own and watch the bottom line, ask yourself whether the organization is making it easy for you to give. Can you give online? Cash or stock? Are tax credits available? Does the organization publish reports with statistics about its success?

If your social impact personality type is a Connector, you'll want to focus on the human side of the equation. Do you know the people involved with the organization, or have you attended one of the organization's events? Have you been personally involved with this organization, either as a volunteer or on its board of directors? Does the organization have the endorsement of a respected third party?

Finally, if you're an Activator who is passionate about addressing a specific community challenge, you'll want to make sure you care about the problem this organization is trying to solve. Does a quick glance at the charity's website give you a sense of how the charity measures outcomes? Does the organization's website include feedback from the people whom the organization serves?

This simple checklist—based on your own social impact style—can cut your decision-processing time in half, and give you a lot more satisfaction from your charitable giving this holiday season, too.

● ● ●

Donor-Advised Funds for Graduates: Give a Boost to Tomorrow's Philanthropists

What's hot when it comes to gifts for the college graduate? You guessed it. Once again, the ever-popular, flexible, and tax-effective donor-advised fund carries the day. This year, more and more parents and grandparents across the country are giving a graduating child or grandchild a donor-advised fund, pre-established and pre-funded, in the name of the graduate.

Donor-advised funds as gifts to the next generation are on the rise at innovative community foundations, financial institutions, universities, and other donor-advised fund providers. "We're inviting our donors to consider 'gift funds' as a way to engage their own family members in philanthropic values," said a community foundation CEO. "We help the donor create the fund, including online access, so that the donor can literally 'put a bow' on the fund establishing document—rolled up like a diploma. The donor adds a card with the website and login credentials, and presents it to the child or grandchild as a gift. Both giver and receiver love the experience."

To make it even sweeter, thanks to today's cutting-edge technology, the parent or grandparent can set up a donor-advised fund for multiple adult children or grandchildren and pre-invite all of them to a "group." Then, when a child or grandchild logs in to see the new donor-advised fund for the first time, he or she is greeted with a personal message from the parent or grandparent.

"Many families consider family content to be a key part of the online philanthropy experience," commented the founder of a Kansas City-based RIA. "This way, the family's values stay intact across generations." Keeping in touch online is key. Families are becoming increasingly reliant on a donor-advised fund platform to share stories about the joy of giving based on personal experience. Some families even share a list of favorite charities that have meant the most to the family over the years. "Telling stories and sharing experiences is itself a gift," added the founder, "because what our clients' families want more than anything is positive communication among family members, especially as children grow up, graduate, and move away."

Family communication is always a plus, and communication across the generations is even richer when it's focused on a topic like philanthropy. Intergenerational dialogue is a major advantage of selecting a donor-advised fund to anchor a family's emotional connections. Hats off to donor-advised funds!

RESEARCH NOTES & ACKNOWLEDGMENTS

The material in *Do Good, Feel Better* was drawn from various research initiatives led by Laura Wells McKnight conducted over the course of several years, often with partners and collaborators, including, in particular, Ann-Marie Harrington.

Here's the research hypothesis we pursued for this book: *Unlocking the secrets in the overlap between philanthropy and psychology produces a useful formula for building positive relationships and personal success, in families, and even in the workplace.*

We'd seen enough in our careers to know that life can be improved by tapping into the power of doing good for others and making yourself better at the same time. As we pursued the investigation into positive psychology and philanthropy, we were heavily influenced by research methods that were both academic and empirical. Our team is rigorously committed to staying on top of trends in the marketplace. We figure out what works with real people, one by one. We are as interested in little data as we are in big data because we believe solutions lie at the intersection of the two. We track behavior through media platforms we create for the purpose of observing employee and consumer behavior. We test ideas. We pilot initiatives. We seek new approaches and alternative strategies for improving the way doing good is experienced by the people doing it, especially employees in companies.

Philanthropy is an important part of American culture. Our intention is to inspire more people, companies, and institutions to realize their own visions of doing good through the best possible personal experience. This, we believe, will in turn increase the effectiveness of philanthropy overall.

Giving to a charity is not the only way to do good. Philanthropy includes a wide range of other activities, including recycling, volunteering, serving on boards, donating canned goods or clothing, attending community events, marketing a favorite nonprofit, sharing with friends and families in need, purchasing brands that support causes, and caring for your own health and wellness.

In *Do Good, Feel Better*, we will show you how the discoveries in our research can inspire you to celebrate "what it means to be human" and help you develop even more qualities that make life worth living.

An extra special shout out to our editor, Kim Schworm Acosta, whose expertise, collaboration, and insights made this book a whole lot better! Kim has been an editor and writer for twenty years, specializing in health, psychology, parenting, and women's issues. Her work has appeared in leading national publications, including *Parents*, *Brides*, *Shape*, *BuzzFeed*, *Family Circle*, *Writer's Digest*, and more. Currently, she is a gift books editor at Hallmark Cards, Inc. Find her at ksacosta.com.

Research Initiatives

Several research initiatives were instrumental in the work leading up to the publication of *Do Good, Feel Better*.

For example:

SOCIAL IMPACT BENCHMARK

Launched in Kansas City in 2015, the Social Impact Benchmark began as a resource for communities across the country. The Social Impact Benchmark operated as a member-driven initiative offering research-based collaboration and educational opportunities for leaders and professionals who embrace best practices for employee engagement and brand enhancement through social impact activities. Interested persons may wish to visit socialimpactbenchmark.com to view the research and publications.

Social Impact Benchmark members include Truss, Bank of Kansas City, Core Catalysts, BalancePoint Corporation, McCormick Distilling Co., Acendas, Spencer Fane Britt & Browne, Jay Mulligan, Certified Financial Planner, Perceptive Software/Lexmark, Mulberry South, Blue Cross and Blue Shield of Kansas City, RubinBrown LLP, Worcester Investments, Forte, Humana, Ceva Animal Health, Bank of Blue Valley, Veracity Consulting, Henderson Engineers, BNIM, Wireless Lifestyle, ECCO Select, EFL Associates/CBIZ, Inc., Two West Advisors, Spring Venture Group, Balance Innovations, Bank of Prairie Village, Missouri Bank, Mainstreet Credit Union, Sunlighten, PGAV Architects, The Miller Group,

JE Dunn Construction Company, One Celebrated, Kimberly A. Jones, Attorney, Tyson Foods, Inc., BNSF Railway, Delta Dental of Kansas, CI Squared, First Internet Bank, Cerner, Two West, Inc. Marketing & Communications, Healthcare Services Group, Inc., McCormick & Company, Inc., W.P. Carey, Inc., and Harper Strategy.

INSTITUTE FOR THE SOCIAL SECTOR

Presented by Kansas City-based Two West, the Institute for the Social Sector was built on the principle that the social sector is a powerful catalyst for economic and community success. The Institute offered opportunities for philanthropic, academic, nonprofit, government, civic, and health care institutions to join together to learn from each other and inspire leadership for positive change. Many thanks to the leadership of Dr. Pat Long, Mary Larson Diaz, and Jackie Kindred in launching the Institute initiative and contributing significantly to its success.

DIARY OF A GOOD GIRL

Diary of a Good Girl was the name of a research-based lifestyle media platform, administered by Mulberry South, LLC, designed to test content and activities related to celebrating good in a household setting. The website operated from 2011–2014 as part of a research study to collect data about consumer trends in philanthropy and social impact. Bolstered by the 2012 publication of Laura Wells McKnight's self-improvement book, *Cereal for Dinner, Cake for Dessert: A True Story to Inspire You to Be Yourself*, Diary of a Good Girl tested strategies to create consumer loyalty through authentic social impact engagement. Allie Flaspohler, research specialist, and Susan Monslow, training specialist, both deserve a special shout out for their dedication and commitment during the early and admittedly messy days of the consumer research.

EAT CAKE, DO GOOD

Eat Cake, Do Good was a 2012 market research campaign designed to test the connection between "celebrating good" and achieving success, both at home and in the workplace. The study connected the dots between traditional notions of philanthropy and principles of positive psychology. The Eat Cake, Do Good campaign included a series of employer-sponsored workshops for employees to learn the basics of philanthropy, charitable giving, social impact lifestyle, corporate citizenship, and community engagement as pillars of personal and professional growth. The campaign featured whimsical cakes—both in print and in edible form—as a metaphor for celebrating philanthropy in the ways that mean the most to the people doing the good. The research indicated that making a positive difference in the lives of others is one of the best ways to make a positive difference in your own life, too. (Note: We still love cake.)

LIVE WITH RINK AND LAURA

From 2011 to 2015, the *Live with Rink and Laura* radio show aired every Tuesday afternoon at 1:00 p.m. on 1660 AM, KMBZ's Business Channel in Kansas City. The show featured co-hosts Ryan Rink and Laura Wells McKnight, together with live guests who shared their personal experiences with the companies they lead, including celebrating achievements, telling the stories behind how they got there and forecasting goals for the future. Each show's guest was unique, but all of the guests shared a common talent for leading the most innovative and successful companies in the Kansas City region, building strong businesses, and doing good in their companies and in the community. You can still listen to the shows at livewithrinkandlaura.com.

CENTER FOR MINDFUL DEVELOPMENT, PLLC

Our research for *Do Good, Feel Better* was substantially aided by Dr. Caroline Hexdall, a licensed psychologist in North Carolina. Dr. Hexdall is the founder of the Center for Mindful Development, PLLC, at mindfuldevelopment.com. The Center is dedicated to providing psychological services and mindfulness education to all children, adolescents, and families. Dr. Hexdall is also pursuing research at the unexplored intersection between the disciplines of positive psychology and philanthropy. Her current areas of study focus on how the combined dynamic of psychology and philanthropy plays out in families to promote healthy relationships. Dr. Hexdall is also involved in building innovative, research-based tools to celebrate philanthropy in the workplace to build a positive employee culture, which ultimately positively impacts families. Dr. Hexdall is an avid photographer. "For me," says Dr. Hexdall, "photography is a visual expression of mindfulness. Taking a photograph means you see the gift of the moment before you, just as it is, without changing it. Photography is a way of honoring each moment for its joyful simplicity. When you stop to recognize the gifts in front of you, you really do see they are abundant."

BOOKS

Numerous books have been written with advice for donors on how to be high-impact social entrepreneurs and, therefore, more effective philanthropists. We found the following to be particularly helpful in our research:

Arrillaga-Andreessen, Laura. *Giving 2.0: Transform Your Giving and Our World.* (2011).

Bornstein, David. *How to Change the World: Social Entrepreneurs and the Power of New Ideas.* (2004).

Brest, Paul and Hal Harvey. *Money Well Spent: A Strategic Plan for Smart Philanthropy.* (2008).

Bronfman, Charles and Jeffrey Solomon. *The Art of Giving: Where the Soul Meets a Business Plan.* (2010).

Crutchfield, Leslie, John Kania, and Mark Kramer. *Do More

Than Give: The Six Practices of Donors Who Change the World. (2011).

Friedman, Eric. *Reinventing Philanthropy: A Framework for More Effective Giving.* (2013).

Gary, Tracy, Kim Klein and Suze Orman. *Inspired Philanthropy: Your Step-by-Step Guide to Creating a Giving Plan and Leaving a Legacy.* (2008).

Tierney, Thomas J. and Joel L. Fleishman. *Give Smart: Philanthropy that Gets Results.* (2011).

KEY SOURCES

- Bureau of Labor Statistics
- Center on Wealth and Philanthropy
- Congressional Research Service
- Giving USA 2015
- Independent Sector
- Internal Revenue Service—Statistics of Income Tax Statistics: Split-Interest Tax Statistics
- National Philanthropic Trust—Donor-Advised Fund Market Report 2014
- The Center on Philanthropy at Indiana University
- The Charitable Giving Report, derived from The Blackbaud Index
- The Chronicle of Philanthropy

- The Corporation for National and Community Service
- The Foundation Center
- The Urban Institute, National Center for Charitable Statistics, U.S. Non Profit Sector
- The 2010 Bank of America Study of High Net Worth Philanthropy conducted by the Center on Philanthropy at Indiana University
- The 2014 Bank of America Study of High Net Worth Philanthropy conducted by the Center on Philanthropy at Indiana University

LITERATURE REVIEW

Finally, this book draws heavily from other scholars' research, including the sources cited below. The author is grateful for the extensive written works, conversations, and practical applications of the many people involved in providing the inspiration for this book.

America's Charities 2015 Snapshot. https://www.charities. org/snapshot2015 Accessed Oct 2016.

American Institute of Philanthropy—CharityWatch: http:// www.charitywatch.org/ Accessed Oct 2016.

Anik, Lalin et al. *Feeling Good about Giving: The Benefits (and Costs) of Self-Interested Charitable Behavior.* Harvard Business School Working Paper. (2009) http:// www.hbs.edu/faculty/Publication%20Files/10-012.pdf. Accessed Oct 2016.

Association of Fundraising Professionals: http://www.afpnet.org/ Accessed Oct 2016.

Associated Press. "Haiti gives conflicting counts for quake deaths." Jan 2010. Archived at: http://www.webcitation. org/5vfoMOdng

Axelrod, Clair. Clairification Blog. http://www.clairification.com. Accessed Oct 2016.

Bernholz, Lucy. "6 Biggest Tech Trends for 2014: Technology Trends for Nonprofits in 2014." *Philanthropy* 2173. http:// www.philanthropy.blogspot.com/

Bernholz, Lucy. "How Big Data Will Change the Face of Philanthropy." *Wall Street Journal*. Dec 15, 2013. http://online.wsj. com/news/articles/SB1000142405270230424390457919 7652066923202. Accessed Oct 2016.

Blackbaud. "Charitable Giving Report: How Nonprofit Fundraising Performed in 2013." Presented by Steve MacLaughlin. https://www.blackbaud.com/files/resources/downloads/2014/2013.CharitableGivingReport.pdf. Accessed Oct 2016.

Blackbaud UK: "Psychology of Online Giving." http://www. fundraising.co.uk/news/2013/12/19/blackbaud-research-probes-psychology-online-giving/ Accessed Oct 2016.

Blackbaud. *np ENGAGE Magazine*. http://www.npengagemagazine.com/read/account_titles/173178. Accessed Oct 2016.

Bloomerang Blog. https://bloomerang.co/blog/ Accessed Oct 2016.

Boston College: Center on Wealth and Philanthropy. http://www.bc.edu/content/bc/research/cwp/publications/by-topic/motivation.html (includes links to numerous articles.) Accessed Oct 2016.

Bruckenstein, Joel. "6 Biggest Tech Trends for 2014." Financial Planning Website. Dec 1, 2013. http://www.financial-planning.com/fp_issues/2013_12/6-biggest-tech-trends-for-2014-2687361-1.html. Accessed Oct 2016.

Business Insider. "How the Girl Scouts built their $700 million cookie empire: Incredible growth story is a model for non-profit and for-profit companies." (2012) http://www.businessinsider.com/how-the-girl-scouts-built-their-cookie-empire-2011-3. Accessed Oct 2016.

Center for Effective Philanthropy. http://www.effectivephilanthropy.org/. Accessed Oct 2016.

CF Insights. http://www.cfinsights.org/. Accessed Oct 2016.

Charity Navigator. "Introducing Results Reporting." http://www.charitynavigator.org/index.cfm?bay=content.view&cpid=1526#.UzbokPk7uM5. Accessed Oct 2016.

Charity Navigator. "Where We Are Headed." http://www.charitynavigator.org/index.cfm?bay=content.view&cpid=1193#.Uzbmmfk7uM4. Accessed Oct 2016.

Chronicle of Philanthropy. "Donations to Aid Haiti Exceed $210-Million, Chronicle Tally Finds." Jan 2010. Archived at: http://www.webcitation.org/5vfoLrlfU. Accessed Oct 2016.

www.city-data.com. Accessed Oct 2016.

Committee Encouraging Corporate Philanthropy. "Giving in Numbers" Study, 2011. http://cecp.co/pdfs/giving_in_numbers/GivinginNumbers2011.pdf. Accessed Oct 2016.

Committee Encouraging Corporate Philanthropy. "Giving in Numbers" Study, 2015. http://cecp.co/pdfs/giving_in_numbers/GIN2015_FINAL_web.pdf. Accessed Oct 2016.

"Doing Good Is Good for You." UnitedHealth Group 2013 Health and Volunteering Study. http://www.unitedhealth-group.com/~/media/uhg/pdf/2013/unh-health-volun-teering-study.ashx Accessed Oct 2016.

DonorEdge. https://learn.guidestar.org/about-us/donoredge Accessed Oct 2016.

Duggan, Maeve and Smith, Aaron. Pew Research: Social Media Update 2013. (Dec 20, 2013): http://pewinternet.org/Reports/2013/Social-Media-Update/Main-Findings.aspx. Accessed Oct 2016.

Dunn, Elizabeth et al. *Prosocial Spending and Happiness: Using Money to Benefit Others Pays Off*. Marketing Unit, Harvard Business School (2014).

Ebrahimi, Rob. "How *to Build a Trusted Online Financial Services Company.*" *Forbes.* May 9, 2013. http://www.forbes.com/sites/rodebrahimi/2013/05/09/how-to-build-a-trusted-online-financial-services-company/. Accessed Oct 2016.

eJewish Philanthropy. "Technology Trends for Nonprofits in 2014. *EJP.* Jan 9, 2014. http://ejewishphilanthropy.com/key-technology-trends-for-nonprofits-in-2014/#sthash.7wTIGqvb.dpuf. Accessed Oct 2016.

Flandez, Raymund. "Facebook Tests Donate Button, a Mixed Blessing for Charities." *The Chronicle of Philanthrophy.* Dec 20, 2013. http://philanthropy.com/article/Facebook-Tests-Donate-Button/143719/. Accessed Oct 2016.

Fox, Susannah. "51% of US Adults Bank Online." Pew Research. Aug 7, 2013. http://pewinternet.org/Reports/2013/Online-banking.aspx. and http://www.pewinternet.org/~/media//Files/Reports/2013/PIP_Online-Banking.pdf. Accessed Oct 2016.

FSG. http://www.fsg.org/. Accessed Oct 2016.

"Giving in Kansas City." The Center on Philanthropy at Indiana University. Summer 2009. https://www.growyourgiving.org/sites/default/files/resources/gkccf-p-giving-in-kansas-city.pdf. Accessed Oct 2016.

Giving USA. "The Annual Report on Philanthropy for the Year 2015." Jun 2016. https://givingusa.org/giving-usa-2016/ Accessed Oct 2016.

Greater Good Science Center, University of Calif at Berkeley. http://greatergood.berkeley.edu/topic/altruism. Accessed Oct 2016.

Great Nonprofits. http://greatnonprofits.org/. Accessed Oct 2016.

"Green Research—Annual Sustainability Executive Survey." *Harvard Business Review.* 2012.

Grovum, Emma and Raymund Flandez. "The Big Boom in Online Giving." *The Chronicle of Philanthropy.* June 2013. http://philanthropy.com/article/The-Big-Boom-in-Online-Giving/139965/. Accessed Oct 2016.

Guidestar. http://www.guidestar.org/rxg/analyze-nonprofit-data/index.aspx. Accessed Oct 2016.

Hall, Holly. "Investing in Fundraisers Who Cultivates Big Donors Pays Off." *The Chronicle of Philanthropy.* Feb 5, 2014. http://philanthropy.com/article/Investing-in-Fundraisers-Who/144319/. Accessed Oct 2016.

"Income, Poverty, and Health Insurance Coverage in the United States: 2014." U.S. Census Bureau.

Indiana University Lilly Family School of Philanthropy. http://www.philanthropy.iupui.edu/. Accessed Oct 2016.

Ingram, Richard T. *Ten Basic Responsibilities of Nonprofit Boards.* 2nd ed. (BoardSource 2009). http://c.ymcdn.com/sites/www.nelpleaders.org/resource/collection/99B352D4-48D2-4F9D-9453-

CFA5A873AC56/10_Basic_Responsibilities_of_Non-profit_Boards.pdf Accessed Oct 2016.

Int. J. Nonprofit Volunteer. Sect. Mark. 16 (2011):342–355. Published online in Wiley Online Library (wileyonlinelibrary.com) DOI: 10.1002/nvsm.432

Johnson, Eric M. McKinsey Voices. http://voices.mckinseyonsociety.com/debunking-the-myths-of-why-we-give/ Accessed Oct 2016.

Joint Committee on Taxation, Present Law and Background Relating to the Federal Tax Treatment of Charitable Contributions (JCX-4-13). Feb 11, 2013. www.jct.gov.

Kansas City, Missouri Commission on Violent Crime Executive Summary. http://ww4.kcmo.org/humrel/aim4peace/exec-summary.pdf. Accessed Oct 2016.

Kopf, Aleese. "KC Keeps on Giving." *The Kansas City Star.* June 19, 2011, A1.

Laura Arrillaga-Andreessen Foundation: http://laaf.org/ Accessed Oct 2016.

"Laws that Encourage the Triple Bottom Line." *Knowledge Leadership.* Feb 18, 2011. http://www.conecomm.com/insights-blog/laws-that-encourage-the-triple-bottom-line. Accessed Oct 2016.

Markets for Good. http://www.marketsforgood.org/. Accessed Oct 2016.

Mesch, Debra. "The Gender Gap in Charitable Giving." *The Wall Street Journal.* Feb 1, 2016. http://www.wsj.com/articles/the-gender-gap-in-charitable-giving-1454295689. Accessed Oct 2016.

Mesch, Debra J. "Women Give 2010." Women's Philanthropy Institute at the Center on Philanthropy at Indiana University, Oct 2010. https://philanthropy.iupui.edu/files/file/women_give_2010_report.pdf Accessed Oct 2016.

Money for Good Study. (2015). http://www.cambercollective.com/moneyforgood. Accessed Oct 2016.

Money for Good Study I. (2010). http://www.hopeconsulting.us/wordpress/wp-content/uploads/2013/04/MoneyForGood_I.pdf. Accessed Jun 2014.

Money for Good Study II. (2011). http://www.hopeconsulting.us/wordpress/wp-content/uploads/2013/04/MoneyForGood_II_Full1.pdf. Accessed Jun 2014.

Narcotics & Vice Quarterly. Kansas City, Missouri Police Department, 1st Quarter. (2011).

National Center for Family Philanthropy. http://www.ncfp.org/. Accessed Oct 2016.

Network for Good, NonProfit Marketing Blog. http://www.nonprofitmarketingblog.com/

Network for Good. *The Online Giving Study: A Call to Reinvent Donor Relationships.* 2010: http://www.fundraising123.org/files/Community/Online_Giving_Study_2010.pdf. Accessed Oct 2016.

Nomensa Blog: http://www.nomensa.com/blog/. Accessed Oct 2016.

Okasha, Samir. "Biological Altruism." *The Stanford Encyclopedia of Philosophy.* (Fall 2013 ed., Edward N. Zalta (ed.). http://plato.stanford.edu/archives/fall2013/entries/altruism-biological/ Accessed Oct 2016.

O'Keefe, Linda Novick. "Doing Good Is Good for Business— Corporate Social Responsibility in 2015." *Huffington Post.* Feb 12, 2015. http://www.huffingtonpost.com/linda-novick-okeefe/doing-good-is-good-for-bu_b_6369242.html. Accessed Oct 2016.

O'Keefe, Linda Novick. "Social Ethics: A Peek into 2012." *Huffington Post.* Jun 4, 2012. http://www.huffingtonpost.com/linda-novick-okeefe/corporate-social-responsibility_b_1401187.html. Accessed Oct 2016.

Pew Research. "Three Technological Revolutions: Broadband, Mobile and Social." http://pewinternet.org/Trend-Data-(Adults)/Online-Activites-Total.aspx. Accessed Oct 2016.

Prince, R.A., File, K.M., & Gillespie, J.E. "Philanthropic styles: A benefit segmentation of major donors." *Nonprofit Management and Leadership.* 3(3): 255-268. (1993).

Pulizzi, Joe. Content Marketing Institute. *Nonprofit Content Marketing Research: Successes and Challenges.* Nov 14, 2013. http://contentmarketinginstitute.com/2013/11/nonprofit-2014-content-marketing-research/. Accessed Oct 2016.

Rytting, Marvin et al. "Psychological Type and Philanthropic Styles." *Journal of Psychological Type.* Vol. 30. (1994).

Schervish, Paul G. "The Material Horizons of Philanthropy: New Directions for Money and Motives." *Understanding the Needs of Donors: The Supply-Side of Charitable Giving.* Eugene R. Tempel and Dwight F. Burlingame (eds.). *New Directions for Philanthropic Fundraising.* 29 (2000): 5-16.

Schervish, Paul G. and John J. Havens. "The New Physics of Philanthropy: The Supply-Side Vectors of Charitable Giving. Part 1: The Material Side of the Supply Side." *The Case Intern. J. of Ed. Advancement.* 2.2 (Nov. 2001).

Schulte, Brigid. "Millennials are actually more generous than anybody realizes." *Washington Post.* Jun 24, 2015. https://www.washingtonpost.com/news/wonk/wp/2015/06/24/millennials-are-actually-more-generous-than-anybody-realizes/. Accessed Oct 2016.

Smith, Aaron. "Real Time Charitable Giving." Pew Research Center. Jan 12, 2012. http://www.pewinternet.org/2012/01/12/real-time-charitable-giving/. Accessed Oct 2016.

Smith, Ray. "A Closet Filled With Regrets: The Clothes Seemed Great in the Store; Why People Regularly Wear Just 20% of Their Wardrobe." *The Wall Street Journal.* Apr 17, 2013. http://www.wsj.com/articles/SB10001424127887324240804578415002232186418. Accessed Oct 2016.

Spacey, Kevin and James MacTaggart Speech. http://www.telegraph.co.uk/culture/tvandradio/10260895/Kevin-Spacey-James-MacTaggart-Memorial-Lecture-in-full.html Accessed Oct 2016.

Starke, Debbie. "What Does Charitable Giving Look Like?" Debbie Starke, Giving Better Blog, April 15, 2011. https://www.growyourgiving.org/giving-blog/what-does-charitable-giving-look. Accessed Oct 2016.

Tempel, Eugene R. (ed.). "Understanding Donor Dynamics: The Organizational Side of Charitable Giving." *New Directions for Philanthropic Fundraising*. 32 (Summer 2001).

Tempel, Eugene R. and Dwight F. Burlingame (eds.) *Understanding the Needs of Donors: The Supply Side of Charitable Giving. New Directions for Philanthropic Fundraising*. 29 (Fall 2000). (J-B PF Single Issue Philanthropic Fundraising) [Paperback].

The Bridgespan Group. http://www.bridgespan.org/Home.aspx. Accessed Oct 2016.

The Center on Philanthropy at Indiana University. "Understanding Donor Motivations for Giving." Oct 20, 2009. http://www.smart-giving.com/plannedgivingblogger/wp-content/uploads/2010/06/Understanding-Donor-Motivations.pdf. Accessed Oct 2016.

The Nonprofit Marketplace: Bridging the Information Gap in Philanthropy. (2008). http://www.givingmarketplaces.org/materials/whitepaper.pdf. Accessed Jun 2014.

Tonin, Mirco and Michael Vlassopoulos. "Corporate Philanthropy and Productivity: Evidence from an Online Real Effort Experiment." *Management Science.* (2014). 141223041315002 DOI: 10.1287/mnsc.2014.1985

Tugend, Alina. "Raising Children Who Care in Times That Need It." *The New York Times.* July 4, 2009. http://www.atlanticphilanthropies.org/news/raising-children-who-care-times-need-it. Accessed Oct 2016.

United Nations Office for the Coordination of Humanitarian Affairs. "Haiti: One year later." Jan 2010. Archived at: http://www.webcitation.org/5vfDnYdk2. Accessed Oct 2016.

U. of Penn. Center for High Impact Philanthropy. http://www.impact.upenn.edu/. Accessed Oct 2016.

U.S. Trust Women and Wealth Fact Sheet. 2013. http://www.ustrust.com/publish/content/application/pdf/GWMOL/ARS7ME57.pdf. Accessed Oct 2016.

Van Straaten, Laura. "How the Economic Crisis Changed Us." *Parade.* Nov 1, 2009.

Wallace, David. "Understanding Donor Behavior." *The New York Times.* Nov 9, 2012. http://www.nytimes.com/2012/11/09/giving/understanding-donor-behavior-to-increase-contributions.html. Accessed Oct 2016.

Wang, Cheng et al. "The Roles of Habit, Self-Efficacy, and Satisfaction in Driving Continued Use of Self-Service

Technologies: A Longitudinal Study." *Journal of Service Research*. (2013).

"Wealth gap between whites, minorities widens." CBS News. July 26, 2011. http://www.cbsnews.com/news/wealth-gap-between-whites-minorities-widens/. Accessed Oct 2016.

Westmoreland, Mary. "The Big Technology Trends for Non-profits in 2014." Jan 2014. http://www.nonprofitpro.com/post/the-big-technology-trends-nonprofits-2014/all/. Accessed Oct 2016.

Whelan, Tensie and Carly Fink. "The Comprehensive Business Case for Sustainability." *Harvard Business Review*. Oct 21, 2016. https://hbr.org/2016/10/the-comprehensive-business-case-for-sustainability Accessed Oct 2016.

"Where Does Discarded Clothing Go?" *The Atlantic*. Jul 18, 2014. www.theatlantic.com/business/archive/2014/07/...clothing-go/374613/. Accessed Oct 2016.

Whillans, Ashley V., et al. "Is spending money on others good for your heart?" (2016). *http://midus.wisc.edu/findings/pdfs/1526.pdf* Accessed Oct 2016.

"1st Quarter 2011 Homicide Quarterly." Kansas City, Missouri Police Department. March 31, 2011.

1-3 Giving USA Foundation (2011). "Giving USA 2011: The Annual Report on Philanthropy for the Year 2010." Retrieved from www.givingusareports.org Accessed Oct 2016.

"25 Most Charitable Cities." *The Daily Beast.* December 8, 2010. http://www.thedailybeast.com/galleries/2010/12/08/most-charitable-cities.html. Accessed Oct 2016.

2006 Millennial Cause Study, Cone Inc. and AMP Insights. http://www.centerforgiving.org/Portals/0/2006%20Cone%20Millennial%20Cause%20Study.pdf. Accessed Oct 2016.

"2009 Annual Report." Kansas City, Missouri Police Department, 2009. http://kcmo.gov/cms/wp-content/uploads/sites/2/2013/10/2009_annual_report.pdf Accessed Oct 2016.

2009 Edelman "Goodpurpose" survey of 6,000 consumers aged 18-64 across ten countries. http://www.prnewswire.com/news-releases/despite-prolonged-global-recession-an-increasing-number-of-people-are-spending-on-brands-that-have-social-purpose-65145867.html Accessed Oct 2016.

2013 Deloitte Volunteer IMPACT Survey. http://www2.deloitte.com/content/dam/Deloitte/us/Documents/us-citizenship-2013-impact-survey-skills-based-volunteerism.pdf Accessed Oct 2016.

ABOUT THE AUTHOR

Laura is an attorney and a writer. She currently serves on the executive leadership team at RenPSG, North America's largest independent philanthropic solutions provider. Laura's first book, *Cereal for Dinner, Cake for Dessert*, published in 2012, is a true story to inspire women to think differently about the role philanthropy plays in their lives. Laura is a leading expert on the connection between philanthropy and positive psychology.

Laura began her career practicing tax and estate planning law at the Kansas City firm of Spencer Fane Britt & Browne. After practicing law, Laura held a variety of positions at the Greater Kansas City Community Foundation in Kansas City, Missouri, which is one of the largest community foundations in the country and manages more than $2 billion in charitable assets. Laura served as the foundation's president and CEO for six years until 2012 when she left that position to launch a series of research initiatives and join the advisory board of Crown Philanthropic Solutions, a software company with more than $6 billion in assets administered on its donor engagement platform. Laura served as CEO of Crown Philanthropic Solutions from May 2015 until September 2016, when RenPSG acquired Crown.

Laura has researched and written extensively on the subjects of philanthropy, workplace culture, and community engagement. Her editorials have appeared in publications across the country, including *The Wall Street Journal*'s online WSJ_MarketWatch, the *Downey Patriot*, *Las Vegas Tribune*, *Hawaii Re-*

porter, *Atlanta Journal Constitution*, newsroanoke.com, *Sun-Sentinel*, *Kansas City Star*, NJToday.net, *Sun Advocate*, *Island Dispatch*, *Greater Tulsa Reporter Newspapers*, and the *Roanoke Star-Sentinel*. While serving as president and CEO of the Greater Kansas City Community Foundation, Laura published two white papers on companies and giving back: "The Case for Corporate Social Responsibility: The Power of the Corporate Philanthropy Platform" (2010) and "Demystifying Corporate Social Responsibility: Four Steps to Success" (2011).

Laura earned a degree in philosophy at Trinity University in San Antonio, Texas, where she graduated Phi Beta Kappa. She earned a law degree, with honors, from the University of Kansas School of Law, where she served as managing editor of the *Kansas Law Review*. Laura has served on several boards of directors over the course of her career, including the Mattie Rhodes Center, Mid-America Planned Giving Council, Nonprofit Connect, Kansas City Area Life Sciences Institute, Young Presidents' Organization, National Association of Corporate Directors Heartland Chapter, United Way of Greater Kansas City, American Royal Association, Start Up Weekend, and the Children's Mercy Hospital Foundation. She is the grateful recipient of several honors, including the Kansas City Tomorrow Distinguished Alumni Award.

Laura lives in Kansas City with her husband. They have five daughters. It is never dull!